Vocabulary Skills, G

Contents

Vocabulary Skills, Grade 4, Introduction

One of the most basic elements of reading comprehension is understanding the meaning of words. However, students may not realize that they do not necessarily need to know the meaning of every word in a selection in order to understand what they are reading. They may be surprised to find that through reading, they can actually increase their knowledge of word meaning. The more words students know, the more they will be able to read, and conversely, the more they read, the more words they will know.

Students can use several strategies to help them determine the meaning of unfamiliar words they encounter while reading:
• using context clues
• analyzing prefixes, suffixes, and root words
• looking up unfamiliar words in the dictionary

Vocabulary Skills is designed to help students practice these strategies in order to incorporate them seamlessly into their approach to reading. New vocabulary words are introduced within the context of high-interest readings. Students can use these context clues to determine the meaning of unfamiliar words. Activities are designed to reinforce the use of all word-meaning strategies.

By increasing their word power, students will also increase their scores on standardized tests.

Organization
The book is organized into five units, with five lessons in each unit. In Units 1-4, each lesson consists of a high-interest reading rich in context so that students can determine the meaning of the vocabulary words based on the context of the reading. Each lesson includes vocabulary activities and most contain a dictionary activity. The vocabulary activities include
• analogies,
• antonyms,
• base words,
• classifying,
• compound words,
• crossword puzzles,
• multiple meanings,
• synonyms,
• word groups,
• word puzzles, and
• word webs.

The dictionary skills include
• alphabetical order,
• guide words,
• syllabication, and
• pronunciation.

Each lesson provides a review of the vocabulary words, once again in a context-based approach, and gives students the chance to practice using the vocabulary words in their own original writing.

Unit 5 focuses on word analysis, with lessons dealing specifically with prefixes, suffixes, Greek and Latin roots, homophones, and words from other languages. The book concludes with a fun section so that students have the opportunity to play games with words.

Assessments
Vocabulary Skills uses two kinds of assessments:
• Two overall assessments located at the front of the book cover all the new vocabulary words. One of these can be given as a pretest to gauge students' knowledge of the vocabulary. Later in the year, the other test can be administered to determine students' understanding, progress, and achievement.
• Each unit also has an assessment. These unit assessments can be administered at any time during the unit as a pretest, review, or posttest.

Vocabulary List
On page 3 is a list of all the vocabulary words contained in Units 1–4. You may want to distribute it to students so they will be able to incorporate the words into their writing for other assignments.

Correlation to Standards
The National Council of Teachers of English has stated in the "Standards for the English Language Arts" the following: "Students apply a wide range of strategies to comprehend, interpret, evaluate, and appreciate texts. They draw on their prior experience, their interaction with other readers and writers, their knowledge of word meaning and of other texts, their word identification strategies, and their understanding of textual features (e.g., sound-letter correspondence, sentence structure, context, graphics)." *Vocabulary Skills* helps students achieve this goal by providing strategies for students to comprehend what they read, increase their knowledge of word meaning, and expand their use of context clues.

Dictionaries and Other Reference Books
Students striving to increase their vocabulary benefit greatly from having access to dictionaries, thesauruses, and other books dealing with word meanings and origins. These resources should be readily available to students at all times.

Vocabulary List

abandoned (2)
acknowledges (19)
acres (9)
adapt (11)
ad-lib (20)
advise (19)
appeal (8)
artificial (18)
assured (8)
avoided (10)

bountiful (19)
brand (5)
breeds (2)

cast (14)
cautiously (6)
choreography (17)
citizenship (7)
companion (2)
composed (18)
considerate (19)
constantly (18)
content (11)
convinced (7)
coral reefs (13)
cowering (10)
custom (8)

debut (17)
deed (9)
delicate (18)
determination (6)
device (20)
dignity (17)
distinguished (18)
dreaded (8)

effects (16)
emigrants (7)
enables (15)
endurance (10)
environment (12)
era (3)
erupts (4)
exclaimed (14)
exhaustion (4)
exhibition (16)
exotic (12)
expression (8)

foreclose (9)
foreigners (7)
frontier (6)
fury (10)

gauchos (5)
gills (14)

habitat (11)
hardships (7)
herbs (1)
heritage (17)
hooves (5)
hovering (14)

immediately (12)
immersion (20)
impressions (16)
indifferent (8)
inspiration (16)
intensity (10)
interrupted (4)

jubilation (17)

lantern (9)
lasso (5)
lava (4)
loophole (9)
lumbered (1)

manes (5)
mantle (3)
mesquite (11)
mimics (15)
miniature (8)
mischief (9)
monotones (20)
monotony (18)

nectar (12)
noticeable (15)

obvious (13)
occupations (7)
omit (16)
opportunities (6)
organisms (13)

passersby (2)
praise (19)
preserve (12)
probing (10)
prodigies (16)
prospecting (7)

rambles (2)
ransacked (1)
rare (12)
reel (14)
remarkable (13)
resemble (15)
reside (3)
rhythm (17)
rodents (3)

scrubland (11)
sculpted (3)
sentinel (3)
settlers (6)
sheepishly (20)
shriveled (1)
siesta (5)
silhouetted (19)
skeletons (13)
species (13)
splendid (18)
stalks (11)
stampede (4)
startling (9)
stimulates (16)
stunned (1)
submerged (13)
substance (12)
succeed (6)
supply (6)
surroundings (15)
survival (15)
suspicious (10)

techniques (15)
temper (19)
tempo (17)
translation (2)
triumphantly (20)
trout (14)

UFO (20)
urgently (1)

volcano (4)

wandering (11)
weight (14)

Note: The numbers in parentheses refer to the lessons where the vocabulary words are taught.

www.svschoolsupply.com
© Steck-Vaughn Company

Name _____ Date _____

Overall Assessment 1

Choose the letter of the word that fits best in the sentence.

1. Susan was so surprised by the news that she hardly noticed her _____.
   - Ⓐ surroundings
   - Ⓑ victories
   - Ⓒ parrots
   - Ⓓ champions

2. That particular species was so _____ that Professor Smith had only dreamed of finding it.
   - Ⓐ noticeable
   - Ⓑ mesquite
   - Ⓒ shrunken
   - Ⓓ rare

3. For several weeks after his foot injury, Uncle Paul _____ painfully around the house.
   - Ⓐ lumbered
   - Ⓑ scampered
   - Ⓒ rambled
   - Ⓓ whipped

4. "Help! Ana fell into the pool," shouted Morrie _____.
   - Ⓐ lazily
   - Ⓑ calmly
   - Ⓒ urgently
   - Ⓓ quietly

5. Many people grow fresh _____ in their gardens.
   - Ⓐ rodents
   - Ⓑ brands
   - Ⓒ volcanoes
   - Ⓓ herbs

6. I was so tired that I fell asleep very quickly when I lay down for my _____.
   - Ⓐ snack
   - Ⓑ walk
   - Ⓒ exhibit
   - Ⓓ siesta

7. The beauty of the land along the river was _____.
   - Ⓐ submerged
   - Ⓑ nectar
   - Ⓒ mesquite
   - Ⓓ remarkable

8. To the untrained eye, the king snake can closely _____ the deadly coral snake.
   - Ⓐ content
   - Ⓑ resemble
   - Ⓒ exhaust
   - Ⓓ lasso

9. Meg had to read *The Little Prince* in Spanish for her class, but she couldn't find a good _____ of it.
   - Ⓐ translation
   - Ⓑ exhaustion
   - Ⓒ fleet
   - Ⓓ era

10. Some kind _____ helped me to my feet after I had slipped on the ice.
   - Ⓐ lassos
   - Ⓑ volcanoes
   - Ⓒ passersby
   - Ⓓ sentries

Overall Assessment 1, page 2

Choose the letter of the word that means the same, or about the same, as the boldfaced word.

11. raging **fury**
- Ⓐ extreme joy
- Ⓑ great anger
- Ⓒ small custom
- Ⓓ terrible lizard

12. supply with electricity
- Ⓐ turn toward
- Ⓑ let go of
- Ⓒ provide
- Ⓓ connect to

13. appeal to him
- Ⓐ reveal
- Ⓑ sound good
- Ⓒ leave cold
- Ⓓ seem disgusting

14. a **suspicious** person
- Ⓐ trusting
- Ⓑ innocent
- Ⓒ happy
- Ⓓ unbelieving

15. easily **convinced**
- Ⓐ finished
- Ⓑ branded
- Ⓒ won over
- Ⓓ managed

16. assured me
- Ⓐ respected
- Ⓑ provided
- Ⓒ appealed
- Ⓓ promised

17. source of **inspiration**
- Ⓐ sadness
- Ⓑ encouragement
- Ⓒ choreography
- Ⓓ bounty

18. pictures at an **exhibition**
- Ⓐ show
- Ⓑ expression
- Ⓒ immersion
- Ⓓ movie

19. spoke **ad-lib**
- Ⓐ without a plan
- Ⓑ following notes
- Ⓒ in a hurry
- Ⓓ splendidly

20. rights of **citizenship**
- Ⓐ belonging to a club
- Ⓑ belonging to a country
- Ⓒ belonging to a group
- Ⓓ belonging to a church

Overall Assessment 2

Choose the letter of the word that fits best in the sentence.

1. My dog is the most faithful _____ that anyone could have.
   - Ⓐ confession
   - Ⓑ mantle
   - Ⓒ stampede
   - Ⓓ companion

2. The boy stood still, _____ by the news he had just heard.
   - Ⓐ shriveled
   - Ⓑ stunned
   - Ⓒ blotted
   - Ⓓ sorted

3. Of all the _____ I know, terriers and dalmatians are my favorite kinds of dogs.
   - Ⓐ rambles
   - Ⓑ breeds
   - Ⓒ mantles
   - Ⓓ hooves

4. The _____ stood guard all night, watching over the sleeping town.
   - Ⓐ passenger
   - Ⓑ gaucho
   - Ⓒ sentinel
   - Ⓓ champion

5. The old house had been _____ years before. It had broken windows and peeling paint.
   - Ⓐ interrupted
   - Ⓑ solved
   - Ⓒ visited
   - Ⓓ abandoned

6. Cowboys use a sharp pick to get mud out of their horses' _____.
   - Ⓐ manes
   - Ⓑ hooves
   - Ⓒ gauchos
   - Ⓓ troughs

7. Doctors _____ began working to save the injured man.
   - Ⓐ interestingly
   - Ⓑ foolishly
   - Ⓒ usually
   - Ⓓ immediately

8. The corn plants lay on the ground, dry and _____ by the weeks with no rain.
   - Ⓐ nourished
   - Ⓑ lumbered
   - Ⓒ shriveled
   - Ⓓ enlarged

9. The lioness waits and watches patiently while it _____ its prey.
   - Ⓐ stalks
   - Ⓑ startles
   - Ⓒ mimics
   - Ⓓ gills

10. The animal's color _____ it to hide in the thick brush.
    - Ⓐ prevents
    - Ⓑ forces
    - Ⓒ enables
    - Ⓓ causes

Overall Assessment 2, page 2

Choose the letter of the word that means the same, or about the same, as the boldfaced word.

11. words of **praise**
   - Ⓐ compliment
   - Ⓑ immersion
   - Ⓒ advice
   - Ⓓ disagreement

12. very **delicate** china
   - Ⓐ omit
   - Ⓑ splendid
   - Ⓒ dainty
   - Ⓓ heavy

13. find a **loophole**
   - Ⓐ way out
   - Ⓑ way of life
   - Ⓒ way back
   - Ⓓ way off

14. proud of my **heritage**
   - Ⓐ dignity
   - Ⓑ prodigy
   - Ⓒ background
   - Ⓓ hardship

15. family **custom**
   - Ⓐ usual way of doing something
   - Ⓑ specially made
   - Ⓒ portrait
   - Ⓓ food and drink

16. **prospecting** for silver and gold
   - Ⓐ weighing in
   - Ⓑ probing into
   - Ⓒ scurrying toward
   - Ⓓ looking for

17. great **opportunities**
   - Ⓐ advances
   - Ⓑ chances
   - Ⓒ ports
   - Ⓓ signals

18. **frontier** life
   - Ⓐ beginning of wild country
   - Ⓑ front line
   - Ⓒ difficult
   - Ⓓ settled

19. made a **debut**
   - Ⓐ beginning
   - Ⓑ ending
   - Ⓒ impression
   - Ⓓ decision

20. **silhouetted** against the sky
   - Ⓐ broken
   - Ⓑ shouted
   - Ⓒ erupted
   - Ⓓ outlined

Unit 1 Assessment

Choose the letter of the word that fits best in the sentence.

1. My dog is the most faithful _____ that anyone could have.
   - Ⓐ confession
   - Ⓑ mantle
   - Ⓒ stampede
   - Ⓓ companion

2. The _____ stood guard all night, watching over the sleeping town.
   - Ⓐ passenger
   - Ⓑ gaucho
   - Ⓒ sentinel
   - Ⓓ champion

3. For several weeks after his foot injury, Uncle Paul _____ painfully around the house.
   - Ⓐ lumbered
   - Ⓑ scampered
   - Ⓒ rambled
   - Ⓓ whipped

4. "Help! Ana fell into the pool," shouted Morrie _____.
   - Ⓐ lazily
   - Ⓑ calmly
   - Ⓒ urgently
   - Ⓓ quietly

5. The boy stood still, _____ by the news he had just heard.
   - Ⓐ shriveled
   - Ⓑ stunned
   - Ⓒ blotted
   - Ⓓ sorted

6. Many people grow fresh _____ in their gardens.
   - Ⓐ rodents
   - Ⓑ brands
   - Ⓒ volcanoes
   - Ⓓ herbs

7. The thieves _____ the mansion looking for the diamond necklace.
   - Ⓐ ransacked
   - Ⓑ sculpted
   - Ⓒ volunteered
   - Ⓓ helped

8. The old house had been _____ years before. It had broken windows and peeling paint.
   - Ⓐ interrupted
   - Ⓑ solved
   - Ⓒ visited
   - Ⓓ abandoned

9. Of all the _____ I know, terriers and dalmatians are my favorite kinds of dogs.
   - Ⓐ rambles
   - Ⓑ breeds
   - Ⓒ mantles
   - Ⓓ hooves

10. I was so tired that I fell asleep very quickly when I lay down for my _____.
    - Ⓐ snack
    - Ⓑ walk
    - Ⓒ exhibit
    - Ⓓ siesta

Unit 1 Assessment, page 2

Choose the letter of the word that fits best in the sentence.

11. Before the horse show, the competitors brushed and braided their horses'_____.
Ⓐ breeds
Ⓑ brands
Ⓒ flats
Ⓓ manes

12. With the death of Queen Elizabeth I, the Elizabethan _____ came to a close.
Ⓐ mantle
Ⓑ era
Ⓒ hour
Ⓓ evening

13. The little stream _____ for miles through the mountains.
Ⓐ herbs
Ⓑ replies
Ⓒ rambles
Ⓓ supplies

14. When she was younger, our grandmother used to _____ in Port Aransas.
Ⓐ reside
Ⓑ provide
Ⓒ brand
Ⓓ disappoint

15. Over time, the force of the water _____ the rocks in the river gorge.
Ⓐ tired
Ⓑ stampeded
Ⓒ sculpted
Ⓓ interrupted

16. Overcome by _____, the long distance runner fell to the ground, unable to go any further.
Ⓐ happiness
Ⓑ exhaustion
Ⓒ boredom
Ⓓ passersby

17. The cattle were frightened by the thunderstorm. They began to _____.
Ⓐ brand
Ⓑ nibble
Ⓒ doze
Ⓓ stampede

18. The _____ pouring out of the volcano glowed with an unearthly fire.
Ⓐ rodents
Ⓑ lava
Ⓒ lasso
Ⓓ plow

19. The beautiful meadow was covered with a _____ of colorful spring flowers.
Ⓐ companion
Ⓑ era
Ⓒ footpath
Ⓓ mantle

20. The cowboy swung his _____ several times before letting it fly toward the runaway calf.
Ⓐ bedroll
Ⓑ lasso
Ⓒ brand
Ⓓ sentinel

Maria Helps

Read the story. Think about the meanings of the words in bold type.

Maria was **stunned** when Aunt Tanya
opened the door. "Aunt Tanya," she cried,
"you don't look well! What is the matter?"

Aunt Tanya said, "I guess I've got the
same flu that many other people have now.
I've been too weak even to work in my
vegetable garden. Look at all the **shriveled**
tomatoes on the vine." Maria said that she
knew a woman in the village who could help.
As Aunt Tanya **lumbered** up to her room,
Maria remembered how quickly her aunt
usually ran up the old wooden steps.

Maria reached the woman's house in the village and said **urgently**,
"My aunt must have your help quickly." She then described her aunt's
illness. The woman quickly **ransacked** a cupboard in her kitchen. "These
are the **herbs** that will make your aunt well again," she said. She handed
Maria two small jars filled with the dried leaves of special plants. Maria
thanked her and ran out. She felt good knowing that Aunt Tanya would
soon be working in her garden again.

**Look back at the words in bold type. Use clues in the story to figure out the meaning
of each word. Write each word on the line next to its meaning.**

_____ **1.** moved in a clumsy and heavy way

_____ **2.** wrinkled; dried up

_____ **3.** searched through every part of

_____ **4.** plants used as seasonings or medicine

_____ **5.** astonished; shocked

_____ **6.** in a demanding, serious way

Base Words

Base words are words without any endings or other word parts added to them. Some endings are **ing, ed, s,** and **es**. Sometimes the spelling of the base word changes when an ending is added to it.

EXAMPLES: open   opening   cry   cried
                    step   steps   tomato   tomatoes

Write the base word of each word below. Then, use the base word in a sentence.

1. shriveled _____

_____

2. urgently _____

_____

3. lumbered _____

_____

4. ransacked _____

_____

5. herbs _____

_____

6. stunned _____

_____

Dictionary Skills

The words in a dictionary are listed in **alphabetical order**.
EXAMPLE: paper, paste, pen, pencil

Write the base words in alphabetical order, one word on each line.

1. _____   **4.** _____

2. _____   **5.** _____

3. _____   **6.** _____

Word Wise

| shriveled | stunned | herbs | urgently | lumbered | ransacked |

Choose the word from the box that makes sense in the sentences below.

1. The man _____ up the hill carrying a heavy load.

2. The leaves of the ivy plant _____ after Ava forgot to water it.

3. Mrs. Garcia was _____ to see how much the neighborhood had changed in the last year.

4. The treasure hunters _____ the cave looking for gold and silver.

5. Mrs. Piper _____ called the doctor when her son broke his arm.

6. Teas made out of _____ are very popular.

Writing

Write your own story about a garden and the plants growing in it. Use as many of the vocabulary words from the box as you can.

_____

_____

_____

_____

_____

_____

_____

Name _____ Date _____

Adopt-A-Pup

Read the newspaper announcement. Think about the meanings of the words in bold type.

It's Adopt-A-Pup Week at the Hillcrest Animal Shelter!

Would you like a cocker spaniel, or a beagle, or maybe a German shepherd? We have dogs of all these **breeds**, ready to join your family. Some of them were pets whose families moved away. Others were **abandoned** beside the road, where **passersby** found them and brought them to us. Any one of them would make a wonderful friend and **companion** for a loving owner.

The Hillcrest Animal Shelter is on Willow Lane, the long dirt road that **rambles** along the riverbank. We are open every day. Come and visit us during Adopt-a-Pup Week. A wagging tail needs no **translation**. It means, "I want to be your pet!"

Look back at the words in bold type. Use clues in the announcement to figure out the meaning of each word. Write each word on the line next to its meaning.

_____ **1.** the changing of something from one language to another

_____ **2.** particular types of animals

_____ **3.** people who travel beside a place

_____ **4.** wanders

_____ **5.** left alone

_____ **6.** someone who spends time with another

A Crossword Puzzle

Use the clues and the words in the box to complete the crossword puzzle.

companion   rambles   abandoned   passersby   breeds   translation

Across

1. people going by a place

4. a friend

6. particular types

Down

2. left alone

3. wanders

5. a change in language

Word Wise

rambles   passersby   breeds   companion   translation   abandoned

Rewrite each sentence. Use one of the words from the box in place of a word or phrase in the sentence.

1. The people going by had no idea what treasures lay inside the dusty bookstore.

_____

2. The house had been left vacant for many years.

_____

3. Many different kinds of dogs were at the dog show.

_____

4. The morning glory vine wanders across the porch.

_____

5. His faithful friend remained by his side throughout all his troubles.

_____

6. What kind of change will I need to be able to understand this foreign language?

_____

Writing

Write your own newspaper announcement about a special event. Use as many of the vocabulary words from the box as you can.

_____

_____

_____

_____

A Mountain Home

Read the story. Think about the meanings of the words in bold type.

When I was a girl, I used to **reside** in the mountains. The peaks had been formed in a long-ago **era**. Over thousands of years, the mountains had been **sculpted** by glaciers into rough shapes. One very tall peak stood like a **sentinel** looking out over the land. Many kinds of animals lived there, from huge elk to tiny **rodents**. The mountains were most beautiful to me when they were covered with a **mantle** of snow.

Look back at the words in bold type. Use clues in the story to figure out the meaning of each word. Write each word on the line next to its meaning.

_____ **1.** guide or watcher

_____ **2.** sharp-toothed mammals, such as mice

_____ **3.** period of time

_____ **4.** carved; shaped; molded

_____ **5.** anything that covers or hides

_____ **6.** live in a place

Name _____   Date _____

Synonyms

A **synonym** is a word that has the same, or almost the same, meaning as another word.
EXAMPLES: small—little   like—enjoy   busy—active

Write the letter of the synonym beside each word.

_____ **1.** era   **A.** live

_____ **2.** mantle   **B.** period

_____ **3.** reside   **C.** carved

_____ **4.** rodents   **D.** guard

_____ **5.** sculpted   **E.** mice

_____ **6.** sentinel   **F.** cape

Dictionary Skills

Guide words are at the top of each page in a dictionary. Guide words tell the first and last entry words listed on the page. Every word listed on the page comes between the guide words.
EXAMPLE: Guide words: **whip**   **who**
Entry words on page: whirl, whisk, whisper, white

Darken the circle for the correct answer.

1. Which word would be between the guide words *script* and *sea*?
Ⓐ sculpt   Ⓑ sentinel   Ⓒ seal   Ⓓ scream

2. Which word would be between the guide words *rocky* and *romance*?
Ⓐ reside   Ⓑ rodent   Ⓒ rocket   Ⓓ research

3. Which word would be between the guide words *epic* and *erode*?
Ⓐ escort   Ⓑ error   Ⓒ envy   Ⓓ era

Word Wise

reside   sculpted   era   sentinel   rodents   mantle

Choose the word from the box that makes sense in the sentences below.

1. Many tiny _____ live in the forest.

2. I would like to _____ in a house by the ocean.

3. The artist _____ a statue of the hero of the town.

4. The statue stood like a _____ guarding the entrance to the city.

5. Hidden under the _____ of night, the owl hunted its prey.

6. During the Jurassic _____, dinosaurs roamed the earth.

Writing

Write your own story about a place you used to live or would like to live. Use as many of the vocabulary words from the box as you can.

_____

_____

_____

_____

_____

_____

_____

_____

_____

_____

Volcano!

Read the story. Think about the meanings of the words in bold type.

I live in the shadow of a large mountain. About every one hundred years, the mountain **erupts** and blackens the air with smoke and ashes. During the last time, burning pieces of rock burst out of the top of the **volcano**. The boiling **lava** that flowed down the slope of the mountain sent up clouds of steam. A **stampede** of people ran from their homes hoping to find safety near the shore. Rescue workers suffered from **exhaustion** after many days of hard work. Their sleep was **interrupted** by reports of new tremors in a nearby town.

Look back at the words in bold type. Use clues in the story to figure out the meaning of each word. Write each word on the line next to its meaning.

_____ **1.** state of being very tired

_____ **2.** mountain that may throw out hot rocks

_____ **3.** very hot liquified rock

_____ **4.** sudden rushing away because of panic

_____ **5.** stopped by breaking in

_____ **6.** throws out hot rocks

Word Groups

Words can be grouped by how they are alike.
EXAMPLE: types of rock   igneous, metamorphic, sedimentary

Read each group of words. Think about how they are alike. Write the word from the box that best completes each group.

> stampede   volcano   erupts   exhaustion   interrupted

1. tornado, earthquake, hurricane, _____

2. tiredness, weariness, fatigue, _____

3. stopped, halted, discontinued, _____

4. rush, flee, run, _____

5. bursts, opens, ruptures, _____

Dictionary Skills

A **syllable** is a part of a word that is pronounced at one time. Dictionary entry words are divided into syllables to show how they can be divided at the end of a writing line. A hyphen (-) is placed between syllables to separate them.
EXAMPLE: dictionary   dic-tion-ar-y

Find each word in a dictionary. Then, write each word with a hyphen between each syllable.

1. lava _____

2. stampede _____

3. erupts _____

4. volcano _____

5. exhaustion _____

6. interrupted _____

Name _____   Date _____

Word Wise

exhaustion   stampede   interrupted   volcano   erupts   lava

Choose the word from the box that makes sense in the sentences below.

1. We were afraid the cattle would _____ during the thunderstorm.

2. In some places, you can watch the _____ flow down the mountain.

3. After a long night with no sleep, the student was in a state of _____.

4. The audience watching the cartoon often _____ into laughter.

5. The ringing of the phone _____ our dinner.

6. The _____ began spewing out ash, smoke, and dust.

Writing

Write your own story about an exciting event. Use as many of the vocabulary words from the box as you can.

_____

_____

_____

_____

_____

_____

_____

_____

Argentina Adventure

Read the story. Think about the meanings of the words in bold type.

I heard the clattering of **hooves** on the hard dirt road long before I saw the horses. The two **gauchos** got off their horses and welcomed me to the ranch. They asked me what kind of work I wanted to do. I told them that I would be good at feeding the horses and brushing their **manes**. The gauchos looked at each other, and one of them asked me if I could use a **lasso** to capture a runaway horse. The other asked me if I would be able to put a **brand** on the three new horses they had brought back with them. I had the feeling that after a relaxing **siesta** in the shade, my adventure in Argentina was about to begin.

Look back at the words in bold type. Use clues in the story to figure out the meaning of each word. Write each word on the line next to its meaning.

_____   **1.** a mark made on an animal with a hot iron

_____   **2.** cowhands of the South American plains

_____   **3.** long hair on the necks of some animals

_____   **4.** afternoon nap

_____   **5.** long rope with a loop at the end

_____   **6.** hard coverings on the feet of some animals

Analogies

An **analogy** shows how two words go together in the same way as two other words.
EXAMPLE: Kitten is to cat as puppy is to dog.

Think about how the words in the first pair go together. Write the word from the box to complete the analogy.

hooves	gaucho	mane	lasso	brand	siesta

1. Person is to feet as cow is to _____.

2. Firefighter is to hose as cowhand is to _____.

3. Bread is to tortilla as nap is to _____.

4. Tattoo is to man as _____ is to horse.

5. Grande is to big as _____ is to cowhand.

6. There is to their as main is to _____.

Dictionary Skills

A dictionary can help you find out how to say, or pronounce, a word. A dictionary has a **pronunciation key** that lists the symbols for each sound. It also gives a familiar word in which the sound is heard. A pronunciation key usually appears on every other page of the dictionary.

a	add	i	it	o͝o	took	oi	oil
ā	ace	ī	ice	o͞o	pool	ou	pout
â	care	o	odd	u	up	ng	ring
ä	palm	ō	open	û	burn	th	thin
e	end	ô	order	yo͞o	fuse	t̶h̶	this
ē	equal					zh	vision

ə = { a in *above*   e in *sicken*   i in *possible*
      { o in *melon*   u in *circus*

Example: adventure (ad ven´ chər)

Go on to the next page.

Use the pronunciation key to help you say the vocabulary words in parentheses ( ) in the sentences below. Write the regular spelling for each word in ( ).

1. We could tell who the cow belonged to by checking the (brand). _____

2. It has been my dream to visit a ranch to see a (gou´ chō) in action. _____

3. The horse lost the shoe off its (hoof). _____

4. He used the (las´ ō) to catch the cow. _____

5. I was careful to brush the horse's (mān). _____

6. After a brief (sē es´ tə), I felt refreshed. _____

Word Wise

Write a vocabulary word next to each definition. Then, use the numbered letters to answer the question, "Where is the best place to see gauchos?"

1. a long rope with a loop in the end ____ ____ ____ ____
                                               1

2. a mark made to identify an animal ____ ____ ____ ____ ____
                                               2   5

3. cowhands in South America ____ ____ ____ ____ ____ ____ ____
                                  3

4. the covering on the feet of horses, cows, and goats

____ ____ ____ ____
          4

5. an afternoon nap ____ ____ ____ ____ ____ ____
                         7   6

6. long hair on the neck of horses and lions ____ ____ ____ ____
                                                        9   8

Answer: ____ ____ ____ ____ ____ ____ ____ ____ ____
            1   2   3   4   5   6   7   8   9

Writing

Write your own story about going to someplace unusual. Use as many of the vocabulary words from the box as you can. Write your story on your own paper.

Unit 2 Assessment

Choose the letter of the word that means the same, or about the same, as the boldfaced word.

1. cowering with fear
- Ⓐ cringing
- Ⓑ giggling
- Ⓒ startling
- Ⓓ flowing

2. miniature castle
- Ⓐ towering
- Ⓑ tiny
- Ⓒ custom
- Ⓓ brass

3. full of **mischief**
- Ⓐ bad luck
- Ⓑ good behavior
- Ⓒ trouble
- Ⓓ intensity

4. avoided problems
- Ⓐ stayed away from
- Ⓑ ran toward
- Ⓒ looked for
- Ⓓ foreclosed on

5. interesting **occupations**
- Ⓐ nightmares
- Ⓑ passages
- Ⓒ hobbies
- Ⓓ jobs

6. determined to **succeed**
- Ⓐ trail behind
- Ⓑ do something well
- Ⓒ volunteer
- Ⓓ endure

7. bring the **lantern**
- Ⓐ source of water
- Ⓑ source of pain
- Ⓒ source of happiness
- Ⓓ source of light

8. puzzled **expression**
- Ⓐ way of saying something
- Ⓑ look on someone's face
- Ⓒ type of movement
- Ⓓ a kind of hardship

9. walked very **cautiously**
- Ⓐ carefully
- Ⓑ heedlessly
- Ⓒ rapidly
- Ⓓ suspiciously

10. brave, hardworking **settlers**
- Ⓐ senators
- Ⓑ cowboys
- Ⓒ exhibitors
- Ⓓ pioneers

Unit 2 Assessment, page 2

Choose the letter of the word that means the same, or about the same, as the boldfaced word.

11. easily **convinced**
- Ⓐ finished
- Ⓑ branded
- Ⓒ won over
- Ⓓ managed

12. a **suspicious** person
- Ⓐ trusting
- Ⓑ innocent
- Ⓒ happy
- Ⓓ unbelieving

13. raging **fury**
- Ⓐ extreme joy
- Ⓑ great anger
- Ⓒ small custom
- Ⓓ terrible lizard

14. **assured** me
- Ⓐ respected
- Ⓑ provided
- Ⓒ appealed
- Ⓓ promised

15. **prospecting** for silver and gold
- Ⓐ weighing in
- Ⓑ probing into
- Ⓒ scurrying toward
- Ⓓ looking for

16. find a **loophole**
- Ⓐ way out
- Ⓑ way of life
- Ⓒ way back
- Ⓓ way off

17. class for **foreigners**
- Ⓐ people from the same place
- Ⓑ people with money
- Ⓒ people who like sports
- Ⓓ people from another country

18. **supply** with electricity
- Ⓐ turn toward
- Ⓑ let go of
- Ⓒ provide
- Ⓓ connect to

19. great **opportunities**
- Ⓐ advances
- Ⓑ chances
- Ⓒ ports
- Ⓓ signals

20. rights of **citizenship**
- Ⓐ belonging to a club
- Ⓑ belonging to a country
- Ⓒ belonging to a group
- Ⓓ belonging to a church

Name _____   Date _____

A New Life

Read the story. Think about the meanings of the words in bold type.

Hello! We are **settlers** here in the West. We left our home back East and came to the **frontier** because Father wanted his own land. He says there are many **opportunities** here for hardworking people. While we are clearing the land and waiting for our crops to grow, the forest and stream will **supply** us with food. Living here isn't always easy, but our family has the strength and **determination** to build a farm. We're sure we will **succeed** at growing fine crops. But right now the land is still wild, so we walk **cautiously**. There are bears in the forest!

Look back at the words in bold type. Use clues in the story to figure out the meaning of each word. Write each word on the line next to its meaning.

_____ **1.** favorable chances

_____ **2.** carefully

_____ **3.** people who move to a new area

_____ **4.** a strong purpose

_____ **5.** an unsettled area

_____ **6.** to do something well

_____ **7.** provide

Multiple Meanings

Some words have more than one meaning. You can use clues in the sentence to tell which meaning the word has.

EXAMPLE: produce

meaning A: fresh fruit and vegetables. We bought **produce** at the market.

meaning B: to bring forth. We watched the magician **produce** a rabbit out of thin air!

Write the letter of the correct meaning next to each sentence.

succeed

meaning A: to do well

meaning B: to follow

_____ **1.** The prince will succeed the queen to the throne.

_____ **2.** We knew he could succeed and reach his goal.

supply

meaning A: to provide

meaning B: thing ready to use

_____ **3.** A hike will supply us with plenty of fresh air.

_____ **4.** One important supply to bring on a hike is water.

frontier

meaning A: unsettled area

meaning B: anything not fully explored

_____ **5.** In the old days, people traveled to the frontier.

_____ **6.** Now, scientists are expanding the frontier of space science.

Word Wise

| settlers | frontier | opportunities | cautiously |
| supply | succeed | determination | |

Rewrite each sentence. Use one of the words from the box in place of a word or phrase in the sentence. You may use more than one word in a sentence.

1. We drove very carefully to the top of the mountain.

_____

2. We felt as if we were at the edge of civilization.

_____

3. We felt lucky because few people have the chances to see such great views.

_____

4. We had to bring plenty of water and food because we knew this area might not provide us with enough.

_____

5. We were the first people to move to this area.

_____

6. She showed such strong purpose that we knew she could reach her goal.

_____

Writing

Write your own story about living in the pioneer days. Use as many of the vocabulary words from the box as you can.

_____

_____

_____

_____

Name _____   Date _____

The California Gold Rush

Read the story. Think about the meanings of the words in bold type.

Many people came west during the California Gold Rush in the 1850s. They were **convinced** that they could become rich **prospecting**. So, they left their homes and families and moved west. These **emigrants** worked long and hard, but very few became rich. Despite the rough conditions and **hardships** of the mining towns, people came from all over the world. Later, some of these **foreigners** decided to settle in the United States and applied for United States **citizenship**. Not everyone came west to work as a miner. There were many **occupations** in a mining town. For example, people could work as storekeepers, carpenters, or bankers, just to name a few jobs.

Look back at the words in bold type. Use clues in the story to figure out the meaning of each word. Write each word on the line next to its meaning.

_____ **1.** people who leave a place and settle somewhere else

_____ **2.** jobs

_____ **3.** felt very sure about something

_____ **4.** looking for gold

_____ **5.** legally a member of a country

_____ **6.** people from other countries

_____ **7.** sufferings

Name _____ Date _____

Antonyms

Antonyms are words with opposite meanings.
EXAMPLES: long—short   west—east   hard—easy   rich—poor

Match the words in the box with their antonyms listed below. Write the words on the lines.

convinced   emigrants   hardships   foreigners   occupations

_____ **1.** immigrants

_____ **2.** pleasures

_____ **3.** doubtful

_____ **4.** natives

_____ **5.** hobbies

Dictionary Skills

A **syllable** is a part of a word that is pronounced at one time. Dictionary entry words are divided into syllables to show how they can be divided at the end of a writing line. A hyphen (-) is placed between syllables to separate them.
EXAMPLE: conditions   con-di-tions

Find each word in a dictionary. Then, write each word with a hyphen between each syllable.

1. convinced _____

2. prospecting _____

3. citizenship _____

4. occupations _____

5. foreigners _____

6. hardships _____

7. emigrants _____

Word Wise

| foreigners | citizenship | prospecting | occupations |
| emigrants | convinced | hardships | |

 Choose the word from the box that makes sense in the sentences below.

1. The little girl was _____ that there was a monster under her bed.

2. After many years, my father applied for his American _____.

3. Many people thought they would become rich by _____ for gold or silver.

4. There are many possible _____ for a well-educated person.

5. Despite all of the _____, the pioneers settled the west.

6. _____ face many challenges when they leave their native countries.

7. In other countries, Americans are considered _____.

Writing

Imagine that you are a prospector or an adventurer. Write your own story about an exciting, difficult adventure that takes you far from home. Use as many of the vocabulary words from the box as you can.

_____

_____

_____

_____

_____

Great-Great-Grandpa's School

Read the story. Think about the meanings of the words in bold type.

My great-great-grandpa kept a diary about his school days. In those years, it was the **custom** for farm children to attend school only when they weren't needed to help in the fields. Grandpa wrote that the idea of going to school didn't **appeal** to him at all. He really **dreaded** starting first grade, but his older sister

assured him she would take care of him. Most days they walked to school, but sometimes they rode in their own **miniature** cart pulled by a little donkey. Grandpa was **indifferent** to the spelling lessons, but he loved learning to read. I wish I could have seen the **expression** of joy on his face when he read his first book!

Look back at the words in bold type. Use clues in the story to figure out the meaning of each word. Write each word on the line next to its meaning.

_____ **1.** not caring about something

_____ **2.** tiny

_____ **3.** looked forward to with fear

_____ **4.** the look on a person's face that shows his or her feelings

_____ **5.** promised

_____ **6.** to seem interesting

_____ **7.** a usual way of doing something

Name _____ Date _____

Synonyms

A **synonym** is a word that has the same, or almost the same, meaning as another word.

EXAMPLES: diary—journal   cart—buggy   donkey—burro

Choose the word from the box that matches its synonym. Write the word on the line.

expression   miniature   appeal   custom   indifferent   assured   dreaded

1. practice _____

2. attract _____

3. feared _____

4. promised _____

5. tiny _____

6. uninterested _____

7. look _____

Dictionary Skills

The words in a dictionary are listed in **alphabetical order**.
EXAMPLE: read, school, spelling, success

Write the vocabulary words from the box above in alphabetical order, one word on each line.

1. _____   **5.** _____

2. _____   **6.** _____

3. _____   **7.** _____

4. _____

Word Wise

indifferent   custom   expression   assured   appeal   dreaded   miniature

Choose the word from the box that makes sense in the sentences below.

1. Grandfather made a dollhouse, complete with

   _____ furniture.

2. Since he didn't care for either seafood or pasta, he felt

   _____ about the choice of restaurant.

3. The baby's _____ was one of pure happiness.

4. The sales clerk _____ us that we were getting a great
   deal on our purchase.

5. It is the _____ in some houses to leave one's shoes
   at the door.

6. "That long, boring movie didn't _____ to me at all,"
   said Tanisha.

7. "I _____ having to sit through the whole thing!" she
   exclaimed.

Writing

Write your own diary entry about your school day. Use as many of the vocabulary words from the box as you can.

_____

_____

_____

_____

_____

A Startling Discovery

Read the story. Think about the meanings of the words in bold type.

Long ago, the Ogata family packed up everything, moved to South Dakota, and bought some land. They planned to farm the hundred **acres** of land and live there forever. Sadly, they had two seasons of bad crops and ran out of money. The bank threatened to **foreclose** on their property.

One night, three children from a neighboring farm were up to **mischief**. Wandering around the Ogatas' farm by the light of a **lantern**, they found an old mine shaft. They told the Ogatas about their **startling** discovery. The Ogatas owned a gold mine!

Mr. and Mrs. Ogata checked the **deed** to their property carefully. They were afraid they would find a **loophole** that would force them to give up their claim to the mine. But the mine was theirs. The day the first ore was mined, the Ogatas gave each of the three children ten gold nuggets.

Look back at the words in bold type. Use clues in the story to figure out the meaning of each word. Write each word on the line next to its meaning.

_____ **1.** a protective case to hold a light

_____ **2.** a legal document showing ownership of property

_____ **3.** measures of land with a certain area

_____ **4.** a way of getting out of the intended meaning of a law or agreement

_____ **5.** to take away the right to own property

_____ **6.** behavior that may cause trouble

_____ **7.** causing sharp surprise

Compound Words

A **compound word** is a word formed by putting two or more words together.
EXAMPLES: sunrise, moonlit

Join one word from Column A with one from Column B to make a compound word. Write the new words.

Column A	Column B
loop	ship
every	close
head	hole
news	thing
fore	line
hard	paper

1. _____

2. _____

3. _____

4. _____

5. _____

6. _____

Dictionary Skills

Guide words are at the top of each page in a dictionary. Guide words tell the first and last entry words listed on the page. Every word listed on the page comes between the guide words.

EXAMPLE: Guide words: **propel**   **protest**

Entry words on page: proper, property, propose, prosper

Darken the circle for the correct answer.

1. Which word would be between the guide words *starfish* and *state*?
    Ⓐ stand   Ⓑ step   Ⓒ shadow   Ⓓ startle

2. Which word would be between the guide words *acid* and *address*?
    Ⓐ ace   Ⓑ adverb   Ⓒ acre   Ⓓ about

3. Which word would be between the guide words *meter* and *miss*?
    Ⓐ motto   Ⓑ mischief   Ⓒ mister   Ⓓ magnet

4. Which word would be between the guide words *decimal* and *document*?
    Ⓐ dozen   Ⓑ deed   Ⓒ daughter   Ⓓ decent

5. Which word would be between the guide words *language* and *lightning*?
    Ⓐ lantern   Ⓑ lion   Ⓒ lobster   Ⓓ lamb

Word Wise

| deed | foreclose | mischief | loophole | acres | startling | lantern |

Choose the word from the box that makes sense in the sentences below.

1. When we go camping, we take a _____ to help us see at night.

2. The bank tried to _____ on the private campground, but the neighbors all gave money to save it.

3. Everyone in the area thought that the fifty _____ of land should be kept for camping only.

4. The _____ was written so that the land belonged to everyone who had given money.

5. The banker, Mr. Merton, thought it was _____ that people would work together for a common goal.

6. He tried to find a _____ in their plan, but he couldn't find any way to break the arrangement.

7. Mr. Merton kept trying to cause _____, but he never got the land.

Writing

Write your own story about a treasure hunt, gold mine, or camping trip. Use as many of the vocabulary words from the box as you can.

_____

_____

_____

_____

_____

_____

Name _____ Date _____

The Stormy Rescue

Read the story. Think about the meanings of the words in bold type.

Laura hurried through the thicket of trees and bushes, hoping to reach the cabin soon. Suddenly, she heard a crash followed by a sharp cry of pain and **fury**. The cries increased in **intensity** as Laura moved deeper into the woods. After **probing** the underbrush, she found a dog caught in the branches of a fallen tree. She leaned over the fearful, **cowering** creature. The poor animal seemed **suspicious** of the human. Laura **avoided** hurting the dog by lifting the branches carefully. Showing amazing **endurance**, the dog limped behind her to the cabin.

Look back at the words in bold type. Use clues in the story to figure out the meaning of each word. Write each word on the line next to its meaning.

_____ **1.** kept from

_____ **2.** moving away or crouching in fear

_____ **3.** the ability to last

_____ **4.** great anger

_____ **5.** power; degree

_____ **6.** carefully searching

_____ **7.** fearful; not trusting

Word Groups

Words can be grouped by how they are alike.
EXAMPLE: types of vegetation   thicket, underbrush, woods, bushes, forest

Read each group of words. Think about how they are alike. Write the word from the box that best completes each group.

> fury   endurance   cowering   avoided   probing   suspicious   intensity

1. great power, strength, potency, high degree, _____

2. searching, exploring, investigating, feeling, _____

3. hardiness, stamina, continuing power, perseverance, _____

4. dodged, escaped, refrained, kept from, _____

5. doubting, distrustful, watchful, uneasy, _____

6. anger, rage, passion, frenzy, _____

7. shaking, trembling, cringing, quivering, _____

Dictionary Skills

A dictionary can help you find out how to say, or pronounce, a word. A dictionary has a **pronunciation key** that lists the symbols for each sound. It also gives a familiar word in which the sound is heard. A pronunciation key usually appears on every other page of the dictionary.

a	add	i	it	o͝o	took	oi	oil
ā	ace	ī	ice	o͞o	pool	ou	pout
â	care	o	odd	u	up	ng	ring
ä	palm	ō	open	û	burn	th	thin
e	end	ô	order	yo͞o	fuse	th	this
ē	equal					zh	vision

ə = { a in *above*   e in *sicken*   i in *possible*
       o in *melon*   u in *circus*

Example: animal (an′ ə məl)

Go on to the next page.

Use the pronunciation key to help you say the vocabulary words in parentheses ( ) in the sentences below. Write the regular spelling for each word in ( ).

1. Wild animals are usually (sə spish´ əs) of humans.

_____

2. It takes great (in door´ əns) to run twenty-six miles.

_____

3. The crowd yelled in (fyoor´ ē) when the umpire made a bad call.

_____

4. He wished he could have (ə void´ ed) the situation.

_____

5. The (in tens´ ə tē) of the game peaked in the second half.

_____

Word Wise

suspicious	probing	avoided	endurance	cowering

Choose the word from the box that makes sense in the sentences below.

1. The dog was _____ under the bed during the thunderstorm.

2. The rabbit _____ danger by being watchful at all times.

3. The deer had to have great _____ to outrun its enemies.

4. The pet detective knew that carefully _____ every possible hiding place would help find the missing pet.

5. She knew the missing pet would be _____ of strangers.

Writing

Write your own story about rescuing a hurt or abandoned animal. Use as many of the vocabulary words from the box as you can. Write your story on your own paper.

Unit 3 Assessment

Choose the letter of the word that fits best in the sentence.

1. The lioness waits and watches patiently while it _____ its prey.
   - Ⓐ stalks
   - Ⓑ startles
   - Ⓒ mimics
   - Ⓓ gills

2. The beauty of the land along the river was _____.
   - Ⓐ submerged
   - Ⓑ nectar
   - Ⓒ mesquite
   - Ⓓ remarkable

3. Alison had everything she needed. She was _____.
   - Ⓐ hovering
   - Ⓑ content
   - Ⓒ upset
   - Ⓓ obvious

4. The animal's protective coloration _____ it to hide in the thick brush.
   - Ⓐ prevents
   - Ⓑ forces
   - Ⓒ enables
   - Ⓓ causes

5. The _____ of the tiny package was surprising.
   - Ⓐ reel
   - Ⓑ survival
   - Ⓒ trout
   - Ⓓ weight

6. The nature preserve was filled with many _____ of animals.
   - Ⓐ species
   - Ⓑ organisms
   - Ⓒ helmets
   - Ⓓ friends

7. Doctors _____ began working to save the injured man.
   - Ⓐ interestingly
   - Ⓑ foolishly
   - Ⓒ usually
   - Ⓓ immediately

8. "Mario won first prize in the pie eating contest!" _____ Peter.
   - Ⓐ dared
   - Ⓑ exclaimed
   - Ⓒ visited
   - Ⓓ lumbered

9. There were many hummingbirds _____ around the feeder.
   - Ⓐ hovering
   - Ⓑ wandering
   - Ⓒ reeling
   - Ⓓ erupting

10. What a strange _____. I've never seen anything like it before.
    - Ⓐ survival
    - Ⓑ omit
    - Ⓒ substance
    - Ⓓ reside

Unit 3 Assessment, page 2

Choose the letter of the word that fits best in the sentence.

11. It is our responsibility to take care of the _____ for future generations.
- Ⓐ techniques
- Ⓑ reel
- Ⓒ environment
- Ⓓ speck

12. The land Juan inherited from his uncle is not very fertile. It is mostly _____.
- Ⓐ scrubland
- Ⓑ marsh
- Ⓒ acres
- Ⓓ mist-covered

13. Robert was found after _____ in the forest for days.
- Ⓐ moving
- Ⓑ ransacking
- Ⓒ wandering
- Ⓓ hovering

14. To the untrained eye, the king snake can closely _____ the deadly coral snake.
- Ⓐ content
- Ⓑ resemble
- Ⓒ exhaust
- Ⓓ lasso

15. One of my favorite fish is _____.
- Ⓐ gills
- Ⓑ reel
- Ⓒ manes
- Ⓓ trout

16. An animal whose _____ is destroyed may be in danger of extinction.
- Ⓐ era
- Ⓑ habitat
- Ⓒ frontier
- Ⓓ intensity

17. The variety of survival _____ used by animals in the wild is truly amazing.
- Ⓐ environments
- Ⓑ breeds
- Ⓒ techniques
- Ⓓ preserves

18. The little boy _____ his fishing line again and again.
- Ⓐ cast
- Ⓑ adapted
- Ⓒ cowered
- Ⓓ dreaded

19. The Great Barrier Reef is one of the most beautiful _____ in the world.
- Ⓐ coral reefs
- Ⓑ deeds
- Ⓒ loopholes
- Ⓓ exotics

20. The number of small _____ littering the floor of the cave showed that it was the home of a predator.
- Ⓐ flowers
- Ⓑ eruptions
- Ⓒ skeletons
- Ⓓ reels

Habitats for Trees

Read the speech by the nature guide. Think about the meanings of the words in bold type.

Look over here, and you'll see a **mesquite** tree, which is common to this area. Birds nest in its thorny branches, and sometimes a red fox **stalks** nearby, looking for a mouse for its dinner. This is a kind of tree that can **adapt**, or fit itself, to the place where it lives. In this **habitat** there's plenty of rain, so these trees grow tall. In the **scrubland**, where there is less rain, they may be only two feet tall. Can you imagine how you would feel if you were **wandering** around in the hot sun, and the tallest tree you could find was two feet tall? Only a very small animal would be **content** to lie in the shade of a tree like that!

Look back at the words in bold type. Use clues in the story to figure out the meaning of each word. Write each word on the line next to its meaning.

_____ **1.** to change to fit a new situation

_____ **2.** a type of tree with thorns

_____ **3.** hunts or follows quietly

_____ **4.** a place where animals or plants live

_____ **5.** region with small plants

_____ **6.** happy or satisfied

_____ **7.** walking around without any purpose

Classifying

Look at the words in the box. Then, place each one in the group where it belongs.

> adapt   stalks   mesquite   wandering   habitat   content   scrubland

1. Plant word: _____

2. Action words: _____

_____

_____

3. Place words: _____

_____

4. Feeling word: _____

Dictionary Skills

A **syllable** is a part of a word that is pronounced at one time. Dictionary entry words are divided into syllables to show how they can be divided at the end of a writing line. A hyphen (-) is placed between syllables to separate them.

EXAMPLE: sometimes   some-times

Find each word in a dictionary. Then, write each word with a hyphen between each syllable.

1. mesquite _____

2. habitat _____

3. stalks _____

4. content _____

5. adapt _____

6. scrubland _____

7. wandering _____

Word Wise

Write a vocabulary word next to each definition. Then, use the numbered letters to answer the question, "Where might you go if you wanted to see plants and animals in their native habitats?"

1. a type of scrubby tree with thorns ____ ____ ____ ____ ____ ____ ____ ____
                                                                          1   2

2. hunts quietly ____ ____ ____ ____ ____ ____
                                            3

3. change to fit in ____ ____ ____ ____ ____
                              4

4. a place where an animal lives ____ ____ ____ ____ ____ ____ ____
                                                                    5

5. place with poor vegetation ____ ____ ____ ____ ____ ____ ____ ____ ____
                                                                        6

6. satisfied ____ ____ ____ ____ ____ ____ ____
                                        7

7. moving for no reason ____ ____ ____ ____ ____ ____ ____ ____
                                      8   9

Answer: ____ ____ ____ ____ ____ ____   ____ ____ ____ ____
              7   4   5   1   9   2   8   4   6   3

Writing

Write your own story about a natural area you have visited or have heard about. Use as many of the vocabulary words from this lesson as you can.

_____

_____

_____

_____

_____

_____

_____

We Need Plants

Read the story. Think about the meanings of the words in bold type.

Not long ago, concern about the loss of forested lands was **rare**. Now people know how important forests are. Trees give off oxygen, a gas needed by humans and animals to survive. Forests also provide an **environment** that many animals need to survive. Some governments have passed laws to **preserve** forests so that future generations can enjoy them, too.

Concern about all plants is increasing also. People interested in **exotic** plants that they had never seen before went to see them at the flower show. Most visitors were **immediately** attracted to the purple, red, and white orchids. Some people listened to a beekeeper talk about her job of raising honeybees. She explained that flowering plants produce a sweet-smelling **substance** that attracts bees. Bees use this liquid, called **nectar**, to make honey.

Look back at the words in bold type. Use clues in the story to figure out the meaning of each word. Write each word on the line next to its meaning.

_____ **1.** the conditions in an area where things live

_____ **2.** from another part of the world; strange; foreign

_____ **3.** right now

_____ **4.** a sweet liquid found in some flowers

_____ **5.** to keep safe; to protect

_____ **6.** not often seen or found

_____ **7.** the material that something is made of

Synonyms and Antonyms

Synonyms are words that have the same, or almost the same, meaning.
EXAMPLES: forested—wooded   humans—people   survive—live

Antonyms are words that have opposite meanings.
EXAMPLES: loss—gain   increasing—decreasing   never—always

**Read each pair of words below. If the two words are synonyms, write *synonyms*.
If the two words are antonyms, write *antonyms*.**

1. nectar—liquid _____

2. immediately—later _____

3. environment—surroundings _____

4. rare—common _____

5. preserve—destroy _____

6. substance—material _____

7. exotic—familiar _____

Dictionary Skills

A dictionary can help you find out how to say, or pronounce, a word. A
dictionary has a **pronunciation key** that lists the symbols for each sound.
It also gives a familiar word in which the sound is heard. A pronunciation
key usually appears on every other page of the dictionary.

a	add	i	it	o͝o	took	oi	oil
ā	ace	ī	ice	o͞o	pool	ou	pout
â	care	o	odd	u	up	ng	ring
ä	palm	ō	open	û	burn	th	thin
e	end	ô	order	yo͞o	fuse	th	this
ē	equal					zh	vision

ə = { a in *above*   e in *sicken*   i in *possible*
{ o in *melon*   u in *circus*

Example: important (im pôrt´ ənt)

Go on to the next page.

Read each pronunciation. Circle the word that matches the pronunciation. Tell how many syllables are in the word.

1. sub´ stəns	subject	substance	_____
2. nek´ tər	nectar	necktie	_____
3. pri zurv´	prison	preserve	_____
4. ig zät´ ik	exotic	exactly	_____
5. râr	roar	rare	_____
6. in vī´ rən mənt	environment	invigorate	_____
7. i mē´ dē it lē	immediately	importantly	_____

Word Wise

immediately   exotic   substance   rare   environment   nectar   preserve

Choose the word from the box that makes sense in the sentences below.

1. As I was walking in the forest, I noticed a strange, gooey

   _____ on the trunks of some trees.

2. I wondered if its purpose was to help _____ the bark.

3. Or, could it be some _____ and unknown material?

4. Maybe it was similar to the _____ found in beautiful

   flowers that bees used to make honey.

5. It could be that these were _____ trees from far away.

6. I knew _____ what I must do.

7. I must study the _____ to answer my questions.

Writing

Write your own story about a concern you have about the environment. Use as many of the vocabulary words from the box as you can. Write your story on your own paper.

Coral Reefs

Read the story. Think about the meanings of the words in bold type.

Coral reefs are found in warm, tropical waters. Although it is not **obvious** at first glance, coral reefs are living things. These **organisms** can grow up to 7 inches a year. They grow layer by layer as the living coral builds on the **skeletons** of the coral that lived before them.

The Great Barrier Reef, found off the northeastern coast of Australia, is the largest chain of coral reefs in the world. It is **remarkable** for many reasons. Like the Great Wall of China, it is so large that it is visible from space. But unlike the Great Wall, the Great Barrier Reef is alive. Second, this reef is home to an amazing number of animals. **Submerged** beneath its waters, there are at least 400 types of coral, 1,500 **species** of fish, and 4,000 kinds of mollusks. The Great Barrier Reef is truly one of Earth's natural treasures.

Look back at the words in bold type. Use clues in the story to figure out the meaning of each word. Write each word on the line next to its meaning.

_____ **1.** wonderful

_____ **2.** different kinds

_____ **3.** ledges made of the skeletons of tiny sea animals

_____ **4.** remained under water

_____ **5.** easily seen

_____ **6.** bony frameworks

_____ **7.** living things

Word Groups

Words can be grouped by how they are alike.
EXAMPLE: types of animals   reptiles, fish, birds, mammals

Read each group of words. Think about how they are alike. Write the word from the box that best completes each group. One word will not be used.

submerged	remarkable	obvious	skeletons
species	coral reefs	organisms	

1. organs, brains, muscles, _____

2. below the surface, buried, hidden, _____

3. wonderful, surprising, amazing, _____

4. sort, kind, type, _____

5. islands, whales, seaweed, _____

6. flowers, dogs, bacteria, _____

Dictionary Skills

Guide words are at the top of each page in a dictionary. Guide words tell the first and last entry words listed on the page. Every word listed on the page comes between the guide words.
EXAMPLE: Guide Words: **treasure**   **tropical**
        Entry Words: tremendous, trestle, trio, troll

Darken the circle for the correct answer.

1. Which word would be between the guide words *special* and *speech*?
  Ⓐ submerged   Ⓑ species   Ⓒ skeleton   Ⓓ spin

2. Which word would be between the guide words *ran* and *regret*?
  Ⓐ remarkable   Ⓑ reef   Ⓒ ramble   Ⓓ rerun

3. Which word would be between the guide words *observe* and *ordinary*?
  Ⓐ oatmeal   Ⓑ owner   Ⓒ organism   Ⓓ obvious

Word Wise

| submerged | remarkable | obvious | skeletons |
| species | coral reefs | organisms | |

Use each vocabulary word in the box to write new sentences.

1. _____

2. _____

3. _____

4. _____

5. _____

6. _____

7. _____

Writing

Imagine that you are spending the day swimming or snorkeling around a coral reef. Write about what you see and do. Use as many of the vocabulary words from the box as you can.

_____

_____

_____

_____

_____

_____

_____

_____

_____

A Fishy Story

Read the story. Think about the meanings of the words in bold type.

"Wow!" **exclaimed** Mabel. "Look at the size of the fish Mom caught."

Mabel was right. The **trout** hanging from her mother's fishing line was big. It was a five pounder at least. The **weight** of the wriggling fish made the slender fishing rod seem to dance in her mother's hands. Its **gills** opened and closed rapidly as the fish struggled for breath.

As Mabel **cast** her line out, she hoped she would catch a fish soon. The silver **reel** flashed in the bright sunlight as she slowly wound her fishing line in. The line finally came up out of the water, disturbing the dragonflies **hovering** just above the surface of the placid lake.

Mabel cast again and suddenly her line jumped. It felt like a big one. Her heart raced as she set the hook and started reeling in her first fish.

Look back at the words in bold type. Use clues in the story to figure out the meaning of each word. Write each word on the line next to its meaning.

_____ **1.** what a fish uses for breathing

_____ **2.** to throw a fishing line or net

_____ **3.** heaviness

_____ **4.** staying in one place in the air

_____ **5.** a type of fish

_____ **6.** a spool for winding a fishing line

_____ **7.** shouted

Multiple Meanings

Some words have more than one meaning. You can use clues in the sentence to tell which meaning the word has.

EXAMPLE: fish

meaning A: a group of animals that live in water. We eat fresh **fish** at the beach.

meaning B: to pull out. I **fished** some coins out of my purse.

Write the letter of the correct meaning next to each sentence.

cast

meaning A: to throw through the air

meaning B: a stiff bandage made of plaster and cloth

_____ **1.** The boy had to wear a cast on his leg for six weeks.

_____ **2.** The fisherman cast his line far out into the lake.

weight

meaning A: how heavy something is

meaning B: value or importance

_____ **3.** The prime minister gives little weight to the opinions of her advisors.

_____ **4.** The weight of the old iron door made it difficult to close.

reel

meaning A: a spool on which something is wound

meaning B: a folk dance

_____ **5.** The band played reel after reel.

_____ **6.** The reel whirred as the line raced out.

Word Wise

| cast | trout | exclaimed | hovering | reel | gills | weight |

Choose the word from the box that makes sense in the sentences below.

1. My best friend and I love to fish for _____.

2. We _____ our lines into the water.

3. We wait patiently to _____ in our catch.

4. The water is quiet and peaceful, with mayflies _____ lazily near the surface.

5. Suddenly, my friend _____, "I've got one that really feels heavy!"

6. The fishing pole bent under the _____ of the catch.

7. We both laughed when we saw a huge mat of grass and brush caught on the hook instead of a shiny fish with flaring _____.

Writing

Write your own fish story. Use as many of the vocabulary words from the box as you can.

_____

_____

_____

_____

_____

_____

_____

_____

_____

The Arctic Fox

Read the story. Think about the meanings of the words in bold type.

The animal kingdom is full of many wonders. Consider for a moment an animal like the Arctic fox. This animal has several **techniques**, or methods, that it uses to increase its chances of **survival** in its harsh environment. Not every animal could live successfully in the Arctic Circle, but the fox survives partly because of its ability to blend into its **surroundings**. Its coat changes color with the seasons and **mimics** the white of the snow or the brown of the tundra. In the winter, its coat is white, which **enables** the fox to blend in with the white snow. In the same way, its summer coat is brown, allowing it to **resemble** the colors of the summer tundra. When an Arctic fox is crouched on the ice or snow, it is very hard to see. In fact, it's barely **noticeable**!

Look back at the words in bold type. Use clues in the story to figure out the meaning of each word. Write each word on the line next to its meaning.

_____ **1.** copies or imitates

_____ **2.** special ways of doing something

_____ **3.** gives the ability to

_____ **4.** things around you

_____ **5.** easily seen

_____ **6.** staying alive

_____ **7.** look like

Name _____   Date _____

Base Words

Base words are words without any endings or other word parts added to them. Some endings are **ity, ed, ing,** and **ful**. Sometimes the spelling of the base word changes when an ending is added to it.

EXAMPLES:
stable	stability
crouch	crouched
allow	allowing
success	successful

Write the base word of each word below. Then, use the base word in a sentence.

1. survival _____

_____

2. noticeable _____

_____

3. mimics _____

_____

4. surroundings _____

_____

5. enables _____

_____

Dictionary Skills

The words in a dictionary are listed in **alphabetical order**.
EXAMPLE: change, coat, color, crouch

Write the base words in alphabetical order, one word on each line.

1. _____   **4.** _____

2. _____   **5.** _____

3. _____

Word Wise

resemble	mimics	survival	noticeable
surroundings	enables	techniques	

Rewrite each sentence. Use one of the words from the box in place of a word or phrase in the sentence. Make any changes necessary.

1. The powerful flashlight allows Marcus to see into the dark cave.

_____

2. Without a steady source of food, the pioneers had much less chance of staying alive on the frontier.

_____

3. The chameleon is able to imitate colors found in nature.

_____

4. Each animal has its own special ways of training its young.

_____

5. Melinda was completely lost. She didn't recognize where she was in the forest.

_____

6. Even though Joe had spilled his drink on his jeans, the spot wasn't easily seen.

_____

7. The daughters look so much like their mother that sometimes it's hard to tell them apart!

_____

Writing

Write your own short report about an animal that has adapted to its environment. If you like, you can invent an imaginary animal. Use as many of the vocabulary words from the box as you can. Write your story on your own paper.

Unit 4 Assessment

Choose the letter of the word that means the same, or about the same, as the boldfaced word.

1. source of **inspiration**
- Ⓐ sadness
- Ⓑ encouragement
- Ⓒ choreography
- Ⓓ bounty

2. made a **debut**
- Ⓐ beginning
- Ⓑ ending
- Ⓒ impression
- Ⓓ decision

3. **silhouetted** against the sky
- Ⓐ broken
- Ⓑ shouted
- Ⓒ erupted
- Ⓓ outlined

4. **composed** music
- Ⓐ wrote
- Ⓑ cooked
- Ⓒ lost
- Ⓓ forgot

5. spoke **ad-lib**
- Ⓐ without a plan
- Ⓑ following notes
- Ⓒ in a hurry
- Ⓓ splendidly

6. a fast **tempo**
- Ⓐ train
- Ⓑ jubilation
- Ⓒ speed
- Ⓓ dance

7. pictures at an **exhibition**
- Ⓐ show
- Ⓑ expression
- Ⓒ immersion
- Ⓓ movie

8. proud of my **heritage**
- Ⓐ dignity
- Ⓑ prodigy
- Ⓒ background
- Ⓓ hardship

9. very **delicate** china
- Ⓐ omit
- Ⓑ splendid
- Ⓒ dainty
- Ⓓ heavy

10. words of **praise**
- Ⓐ compliment
- Ⓑ immersion
- Ⓒ advice
- Ⓓ disagreement

Unit 4 Assessment, page 2

Choose the letter of the word that means the same, or about the same, as the boldfaced word.

11. artificial flowers
- Ⓐ ad-lib
- Ⓑ impressive
- Ⓒ realistic
- Ⓓ fake

12. a **considerate** person
- Ⓐ delicate
- Ⓑ happy
- Ⓒ sheepish
- Ⓓ thoughtful

13. labor-saving **device**
- Ⓐ exhibition
- Ⓑ idea
- Ⓒ machine
- Ⓓ tempo

14. endless **monotony**
- Ⓐ monotone
- Ⓑ dull routine
- Ⓒ argument
- Ⓓ jubilation

15. award-winning **choreography**
- Ⓐ dance moves
- Ⓑ choir performance
- Ⓒ silhouette
- Ⓓ effects

16. first **impressions**
- Ⓐ looks
- Ⓑ prodigies
- Ⓒ entrances
- Ⓓ debuts

17. moving **constantly**
- Ⓐ all the time
- Ⓑ sheepishly
- Ⓒ once in a while
- Ⓓ now and again

18. stimulates the economy
- Ⓐ improves
- Ⓑ has no effect on
- Ⓒ harms
- Ⓓ advises

19. complete **immersion**
- Ⓐ doodling
- Ⓑ driving
- Ⓒ drying
- Ⓓ dipping

20. terrible **temper**
- Ⓐ tender
- Ⓑ mood
- Ⓒ composed
- Ⓓ acknowledge

Rolando Paints

Read Rolando's description of how he paints. Think about the meanings of the words in bold type.

I am finishing a painting for a museum **exhibition**. I looked at a sunset and then painted my **impressions** of it. I was planning to include a tree, but I decided to **omit** it. I use different colors to create different **effects**. Everything I see is an **inspiration** for my painting. Some child **prodigies** do nothing but paint, but I like to play soccer, too. Exercise **stimulates** my mind!

Look back at the words in bold type. Use clues in the story to figure out the meaning of each word. Write each word on the line next to its meaning.

_____ **1.** results; outcomes

_____ **2.** a force that awakens the mind or feelings

_____ **3.** very talented and brilliant children; geniuses

_____ **4.** leave something out; forget something

_____ **5.** feelings; ideas

_____ **6.** excites; makes active

_____ **7.** presentation; show; display

Base Words

Base words are words without any endings or other word parts added to them. Some endings are **ed, ing, s, ion,** and **ation**. Sometimes the spelling of the base word changes when an ending is added to it.

EXAMPLES:

paint	painted
plan	planning
color	colors
integrate	integration

Write the base word of each word below. Then, use the base word in a sentence.

1. effects _____

_____

2. inspiration _____

_____

3. exhibition _____

_____

4. stimulates _____

_____

5. prodigies _____

_____

6. impressions _____

_____

Dictionary Skills

Write the base words in alphabetical order, one word on each line.

1. _____   **4.** _____

2. _____   **5.** _____

3. _____   **6.** _____

Word Wise

effects impressions stimulates prodigies omit exhibition inspiration

Choose the word from the box that makes sense in the sentences below.

1. The child _____ at the art school are working hard on their projects.

2. The art school is planning an _____ of the student's work.

3. The school staff _____ the students to reach their creative side.

4. The school planners are careful not to _____ a single detail.

5. Artists often look to nature for their _____.

6. A good art program can have very positive _____ on all students.

7. The visitors are sure to leave with very good _____ of the school and its work.

Writing

Write your own story about what you enjoy doing, whether it is painting, singing, playing a musical instrument, or playing a sport. Use as many of the vocabulary words from the box as you can.

_____

_____

_____

_____

_____

_____

Name _____ Date _____

A Native American Celebration

Read the story. Think about the meanings of the words in bold type.

Shane and Carla are attending a dance performance.

"The program says this dance group has never performed before. It's their **debut**," said Carla.

Shane read his program. "It says their dances celebrate their Native American **heritage**," he said. "The first dance is a slow one. It shows the **dignity** of their people."

"I like dances with a fast **tempo** the best," said Carla. "I feel the **rhythm** and want to dance, too."

"Then you'll like the second dance," Shane told her. "The program says the dancers will use fast movements to show their feeling of **jubilation**."

"I wish I could plan **choreography** like that," Carla answered.

Look back at the words in bold type. Use clues in the story to figure out the meaning of each word. Write each word on the line next to its meaning.

_____ **1.** the repeating beat of music

_____ **2.** speed of the beat of a dance or piece of music

_____ **3.** planned set of dance movements

_____ **4.** great gladness or happiness

_____ **5.** traditions handed down from the past

_____ **6.** first public performance

_____ **7.** honor; pride; self-respect

Name _____

Date _____

Word Web

Fill in the word web with words from the box.

| choreography | debut | rhythm | heritage | jubilation | tempo | dignity |

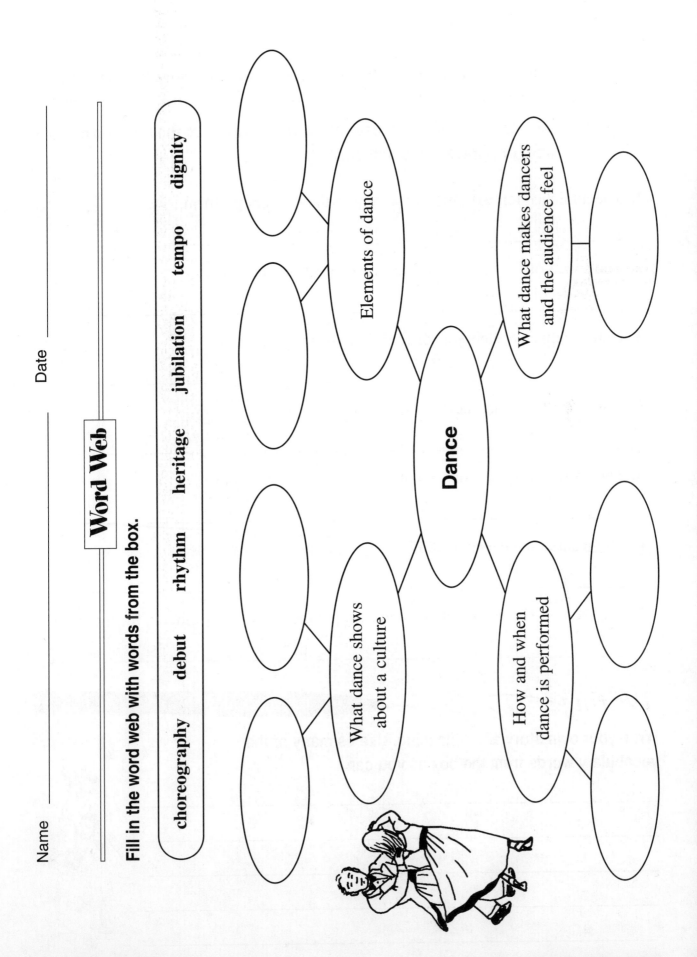

Elements of dance

What dance makes dancers and the audience feel

Dance

What dance shows about a culture

How and when dance is performed

Word Wise

tempo   heritage   jubilation   choreography   debut   dignity   rhythm

Rewrite each sentence. Use one of the words from the box in place of a word or phrase in the sentence.

1. The audience felt extreme joy watching the dancers perform.

_____

2. The speed of the music made us want to get up and dance.

_____

3. Dance helps us celebrate our traditions from the past.

_____

4. It was hard to resist the beat of the music.

_____

5. Tanika was very nervous about her first public appearance.

_____

6. She wanted the dance to show the great honor of her people.

_____

7. We thought she had created wonderful planned dance movements for the music.

_____

Writing

Write your own story about dancing. Use as many of the vocabulary words from the box as you can.

_____

_____

_____

_____

Name _____ Date _____

This Princess Rocks

Read the story. Think about the meanings of the words in bold type.

Once upon a time, a lovely princess lived in a **splendid** castle. Because the princess loved music, her father, the king, hired the most famous and **distinguished** musician he could find to teach the princess to play the harp. She practiced **constantly** and learned quickly. Every day, she **composed** beautiful songs as her **delicate** fingers flew over the harp strings. On a chain she even wore a small harp carved from an **artificial** diamond that looked like a real one.

After many months, the princess grew tired of harp music. "Day after day, it's always the same," she said. "I'm tired of this **monotony**. I need a change. I want to play guitar in a rock band."

And that is just what she did.

Look back at the words in bold type. Use clues in the story to figure out the meaning of each word. Write each word on the line next to its meaning.

_____ **1.** happening all the time

_____ **2.** very finely shaped

_____ **3.** not real; made by people, not by nature

_____ **4.** set apart; famous; outstanding

_____ **5.** the same dull, boring routine

_____ **6.** beautiful; gorgeous; dazzling

_____ **7.** created; wrote

Name _____   Date _____

Antonyms

Antonyms are words that have opposite meanings.
EXAMPLES: famous—unknown   quickly—slowly   small—large

Match the words in the box with their antonyms. Write the words on the lines.

composed	constantly	delicate	distinguished
monotony	splendid	artificial	

1. plain _____

2. ordinary _____

3. destroyed _____

4. rough _____

5. real _____

6. excitement _____

7. never _____

Dictionary Skills

A **syllable** is a part of a word that is pronounced at one time. Dictionary entry words are divided into syllables to show how they can be divided at the end of a writing line. A hyphen (-) is placed between syllables to separate them.
EXAMPLE: musician   mu-si-cian

Find each word in a dictionary. Then, write each word with a hyphen between each syllable.

1. splendid _____

5. monotony _____

2. distinguished _____

6. composed _____

3. constantly _____

7. artificial _____

4. delicate _____

Word Wise

artificial	composed	delicate	constantly
monotony	splendid	distinguished	

Choose the word from the box that makes sense in the sentences below.

1. If you practice _____, you will become an expert.

2. Many songwriters _____ their best work when they were very young.

3. The most _____ musicians win many awards.

4. We spent a _____ day at the beach.

5. We also enjoy going to water parks, even though the wave pools are

   _____.

6. The dragonfly wings were very _____ and glimmered in the sunlight.

7. The time we spent in the water certainly broke the _____ of a boring summer!

Writing

Write your own story about how you would most like to spend your time and what career you would like to have. Use as many of the vocabulary words from the box as you can.

_____

_____

_____

_____

_____

_____

_____

The Kingly Truth

Read the story. Think about the meanings of the words in bold type.

Many years ago, a king needed to decide which of two noblemen he could trust. He summoned them to his castle to test them. As they approached, the dark outline of the castle was **silhouetted** against the moonlit sky.

The king showed the noblemen a set of laws that would have treated his subjects harshly. "Noblemen," the king said, "please **advise** me about these laws. What will my subjects think of them?"

"Your Highness," the first nobleman said, "all your subjects will **praise** you if you issue these laws. These measures prove your **bountiful** kindness."

"Your Highness," the second nobleman said, "if you are not **considerate** of your subjects' needs, how can you expect them to be loyal to you?" The second nobleman gave his opinion honestly, with no fear of the king's **temper**.

After both had spoken, the king said, "The man I can trust is the one who **acknowledges** the truth." He banished the first nobleman to a faraway land and invited the second nobleman to live in his castle as his highest adviser.

Look back at the words in bold type. Use clues in the story to figure out the meaning of each word. Write each word on the line next to its meaning.

_____ **1.** notices or recognizes

_____ **2.** frame of mind; mood

_____ **3.** thoughtful

_____ **4.** express approval of

_____ **5.** give an opinion

_____ **6.** plentiful; more than enough; generous

_____ **7.** outlined against a light background

Multiple Meanings

Some words have more than one meaning. You can use clues in the sentence to tell which meaning the word has.

EXAMPLE: subjects

meaning A: courses of study in school. Of all the **subjects**, science is my favorite.

meaning B: people under the control of a ruler. The king greets his **subjects**.

Write the letter of the correct meaning next to each sentence.

advise

meaning A: to give advice to

meaning B: to inform or tell about something

_____ **1.** The announcer will advise us when the plane has arrived.

_____ **2.** The counselor is here to advise students how to handle difficult problems.

acknowledges

meaning A: admits that something is true

meaning B: shows that something has been received

_____ **3.** He acknowledges that he is not the best player on the team.

_____ **4.** This thank you note acknowledges that the gift had arrived.

temper

meaning A: mood

meaning B: to make metal harder

_____ **5.** A heating and cooling process is used to temper steel.

_____ **6.** The baby was in a bad temper after she missed her nap.

Word Wise

praise	silhouetted	acknowledges	advise
temper	considerate	bountiful	

Choose the word from the box that makes sense in the sentences below.

1. Melvin's headache put him in such a bad _____ that

   he just wanted to go to sleep.

2. Anna always tries to make everyone feel at home, and

   she is very _____ of their feelings.

3. The _____ harvest meant the

   family would have plenty of food during the winter.

4. The movie ended with the couple _____ against the

   beautiful sunset.

5. Everyone will _____ him for such a kind act.

6. Can you _____ me about what I should do?

7. She _____ that sometimes it is hard to tell the truth.

Writing

Write your own story set in a time long ago. Use as many of the vocabulary words from the box as you can.

_____

_____

_____

_____

_____

_____

It's a UFO!

Read the story. Think about the meanings of the words in bold type.

Until yesterday, I never thought that the shining disk I had seen in the sky might be a **UFO**. When the alien approached me, he spoke in **monotones**. He sounded more like a robot than a person. He was convinced that a special **device** I had could help him locate his spacecraft.

Sheepishly, I explained that the thing he described was only an **immersion** heater. It is a metal coil that heats water for hot drinks. I showed him how it works. He seized it, laughing **triumphantly**. Until then, his words had sounded rehearsed. Now he joked, "Don't you think aliens enjoy a cup of hot tea, too?" That's how I learned that he could **ad-lib**.

Look back at the words in bold type. Use clues in the story to figure out the meaning of each word. Write each word on the line next to its meaning.

_____ **1.** in an embarrassed way; shyly; bashfully

_____ **2.** to say something that is made up on the spot and not planned beforehand

_____ **3.** in a way that shows victory and success

_____ **4.** an Unidentified Flying Object; a spaceship

_____ **5.** the same levels, with no changes

_____ **6.** covering something completely

_____ **7.** an invention; a machine; an instrument

Make a Picture

How do you picture words? Sometimes the picture you draw in your mind can help you remember the meanings of words.

EXAMPLE: alien

Draw a picture for each of the vocabulary words below.

1. UFO	**2.** sheepishly
3. device	**4.** immersion
5. monotones	**6.** triumphantly

Word Wise

| triumphantly   sheepishly   device   UFO   immersion   monotones   ad-lib |

Rewrite each sentence. Use one of the words from the box in place of a word or phrase in the sentence.

1. Ben Stein has become famous for speaking in a boring, unchanging way.

_____

2. She soaked her tired feet in a bath where they were completely covered.

_____

3. The young man bashfully accepted the prize for the best apple pie.

_____

4. She knew how to talk without a planned speech about many different topics.

_____

5. When I saw something streaking across the night sky, I thought it might be a ship from outer space.

_____

6. The team returned in great victory after winning the game.

_____

7. That new invention will help people travel more safely.

_____

Writing

Imagine that you have seen an alien spaceship land. Write your own story about what happened. Use as many of the vocabulary words from the box as you can.

_____

_____

_____

_____

Unit 5 Assessment

Choose the letter of the correct answer.

1. Which of the following prefixes can be added to the root word *appear* to make a new word?
   - Ⓐ mis
   - Ⓑ un
   - Ⓒ dis
   - Ⓓ bi

2. Which of the following suffixes can be added to the root word *effort* to make a new word?
   - Ⓐ ly
   - Ⓑ ful
   - Ⓒ est
   - Ⓓ less

3. Choose the homophone that correctly completes the sentence.
   I went _____ the store.
   - Ⓐ two
   - Ⓑ too
   - Ⓒ to
   - Ⓓ toe

4. Choose the homophone that correctly completes the sentence.
   _____ dog is the cutest dog in town.
   - Ⓐ They're
   - Ⓑ They
   - Ⓒ There
   - Ⓓ Their

5. Choose the homophone that correctly completes the sentence.
   _____ are good, but I like apples more.
   - Ⓐ Pairs
   - Ⓑ Pares
   - Ⓒ Pears
   - Ⓓ Pays

6. Which prefix makes *lock* mean "to open"?
   - Ⓐ non
   - Ⓑ re
   - Ⓒ bi
   - Ⓓ un

7. Which prefix makes *draw* mean "to draw again"?
   - Ⓐ re
   - Ⓑ pre
   - Ⓒ in
   - Ⓓ un

8. Choose the word that gives the meaning of the underlined prefix.
   You need to <u>re</u>view the lesson.
   - Ⓐ not
   - Ⓑ always
   - Ⓒ again
   - Ⓓ with

Unit 5 Assessment, page 2

Choose the letter of the correct answer.

9. Which word comes from the Latin root *dict*, which means "to say"?
- Ⓐ desk
- Ⓑ dictate
- Ⓒ did
- Ⓓ doctor

10. Which sentence does the homophone *there* correctly complete?
- Ⓐ Put your bag over _____.
- Ⓑ _____ going to New Jersey by train.
- Ⓒ _____ house is in Lakeview.
- Ⓓ What are _____ favorite movies?

11. Choose the sentence in which the homophone *right* or *write* is used incorrectly.
- Ⓐ I will write my grandmother a letter tonight.
- Ⓑ We went to the movies right after school on Friday.
- Ⓒ Hilary thinks she is always write.
- Ⓓ You have the right to remain silent.

12. Which of the following suffixes can be added to the root word *flex* to make a new word?
- Ⓐ ly
- Ⓑ ship
- Ⓒ er
- Ⓓ ible

13. Which suffix changes the word *harm* to mean "without harm"?
- Ⓐ ful
- Ⓑ less
- Ⓒ ed
- Ⓓ al

14. Which word comes from the Latin word *mater*?
- Ⓐ moss
- Ⓑ mountain
- Ⓒ scared
- Ⓓ mother

15. Which suffix should be added to the word *sing* to form a word that means "one who sings"?
- Ⓐ or
- Ⓑ ly
- Ⓒ al
- Ⓓ er

16. Choose the pair of homophones that correctly completes the sentence.
The dog _____ _____ let go of the bone.
- Ⓐ wood   not
- Ⓑ wood   knot
- Ⓒ would   knot
- Ⓓ would   not

Prefixes

A **prefix** is a syllable added to the beginning of a word to
change the meaning of the word.
EXAMPLES:
The prefix **dis** means "not" or "the opposite of." **dis**appear
The prefix **mis** means "bad(ly)" or "wrong(ly)." **mis**behave
The prefix **re** means "again" or "back." **re**do
The prefix **un** means "not" or "the opposite of." **un**friendly

Complete each sentence by adding the prefix <u>un</u> or <u>dis</u> to the word in ( ).

1. (appear) Tabor the Great made a man _____ from the stage.

2. (concerned) The man looked _____ about what would happen.

3. (aware) He seemed _____ that he was even on stage.

4. (cover) The man vanished! The audience tried to _____ where he had gone.

5. (harmed) But the man reappeared and was _____.

6. (like) It would be hard to _____ an act as great as Tabor's.

7. (agree) No one could _____ with the fact that it had been a fine evening.

Complete each sentence by adding the prefix <u>mis</u> or <u>re</u> to the word in ( ).

8. (understood) I _____ the plan for the park at the edge of town.

9. (use) I didn't want to see a _____ of such fine land.

10. (create) The plan is to _____ our town as it was long ago.

11. (live) It will help us to _____ the history of the town.

12. (judged) I really _____ the plan.

13. (act) I should learn not to _____ before I learn all the facts.

More Prefixes

Remember that a **prefix** is a syllable added to the beginning of a word to change the meaning of the word. The part of the word that the prefix is added to is called a **base** word or **root** word.

EXAMPLE: Julio is happy. Julio is **un**happy. (prefix = un; base word = happy)

Prefix	Meaning	Example
dis	not	dislike
im	not	impossible
mis	incorrectly	mistake
pre	before	prepay
re	back	return
un	not	undo

Read each sentence. Add a prefix with the meaning shown to each underlined word. Use the list above to help you.

1. Seth was <u>fair</u> to keep Sonia's soccer ball. (not) _____

2. He should have <u>turned</u> it to her. (back) _____

3. Sonia is <u>able</u> to understand why he took the ball. (not) _____

4. She <u>understood</u> what he wanted to do. (incorrectly) _____

5. Seth had <u>planned</u> how he would take the ball. (before) _____

6. He waited <u>patiently</u> to see what Sonia would do. (not) _____

7. He wanted to <u>pay</u> her for losing his baseball card. (back) _____

8. When Seth saw how <u>happy</u> Sonia was, he felt sorry. (not) _____

9. He was <u>pleased</u> with the way things had gone. (not) _____

10. Seth <u>turned</u> the ball and apologized to Sonia. (back) _____

Prefixes in Context

Choose the word from the box that makes sense in the sentences below.

unwisely	disappearing	impossible	unfamiliar
unknown	disregarded	return	

At Camp WonderDaze, Jacy decided to go hiking by himself. He knew that he shouldn't go off alone in the wilderness. Even so, he

(1) _____ that rule and left camp without telling anyone. Soon, Jacy realized that he was lost. He had gone into an (2) _____ part of the forest. He was

(3) _____ with his surroundings. The sun was

(4) _____ from view. Jacy wished he could find the

(5) _____ path. He thoroughly checked every item in his backpack for a compass or a map, but he had

(6) _____ left without them.

When Jacy looked up, a wolf jumped into his path. Suddenly, it was

(7) _____ for Jacy to move. As he stared at the wolf, he heard someone call his name, and the wolf bounded into the forest.

Writing

Write your own story about a wilderness hiking trip. Use as many words with prefixes as you can.

_____

_____

_____

_____

_____

Suffixes

A **suffix** is a syllable added to the end of a word to change the meaning of the word.
EXAMPLES:
The suffix **ful** means "full of," "able to," or "the amount that will fill." hope**ful**, help**ful**, spoon**ful**
The suffix **less** means "without" or "not able to do." hope**less**, harm**less**

In each blank, write the word that matches the definition in ( ).

effortless	worthless	meaningful	endless
successful	careless	joyless	tireless

1. Giving a _____ party is not easy. (full of success)

2. When planning a party, I am _____. (not able to tire)

3. If the party is well planned, it looks _____. (without effort)

4. A _____ mistake can ruin a party. (without care)

5. A _____ game helps people to get into the spirit of the party. (full of meaning)

6. There is an _____ number of party games. (without end)

7. But all of the planning is _____ if no one comes. (without worth)

8. It would be a _____ evening if no one came to my party! (without joy)

Write a definition for the underlined word in each phrase.

9. colorless soap _____

10. bottomless pit _____

11. sorrowful event _____

12. beautiful car _____

13. flavorless meal _____

More Suffixes

Remember that a **suffix** is a syllable added to the end of a word to change the meaning of the word or the way the word is used. The part of the word that the suffix is added to is called a **base** word or **root** word.

EXAMPLE: The child is quiet. The child played quiet**ly**.

(base word = quiet; suffix = ly)

Suffix	Meaning	Example
al	like, referring to	coast<u>al</u>
able, ible	able to be	break<u>able</u>, flex<u>ible</u>
er, or	one who	sing<u>er</u>, sail<u>or</u>
ful	full of	help<u>ful</u>
less	without	hope<u>less</u>
y	what kind	snow<u>y</u>
ly	how	quick<u>ly</u>
ist	one who does	art<u>ist</u>
ship	the condition of being	partner<u>ship</u>

Read each sentence. Choose a suffix from the list above. Add it to the word in ( ). Then, write the word in the blank. You may need to change the spelling.

1. It was a dark, (storm) night. _____

2. A (visit) came to my door. _____

3. He (polite) asked if he could come in from the rain. _____

4. The man's (music) voice charmed me. _____

5. He sat by my fire and told (wonder) stories. _____

6. The stories were full of (magic) characters. _____

7. He told of (remark) travels and adventures. _____

8. I told the man his stories were amazing but (unbelieve). _____

9. These incredible things had (actual) happened to him! _____

10. After that night, I felt that we had developed a (friend). _____

Name _____   Date _____

Suffixes in Context

Choose the word from the box that makes sense in the sentences below.

carefully	confidently	successful	helpful	lovable
willingly	partnership	handler	joyful	tireless

Newfoundland dogs have a great talent for finding people. A single, truly

(1) _____ Newfoundland dog saved one hundred people in one

rescue. Hugger was trained by Susie, his **(2)** _____. Hugger, as

his name suggests, is calm and **(3)** _____. He formed a close

(4) _____ with Susie. Only when he is at work looking for lost

people does he **(5)** _____ leave her side. Susie

(6) _____ tells him to do his job. Hugger is

(7) _____ when he is searching for someone. He will keep going

even after many hours. He **(8)** _____ searches everywhere until

he is **(9)** _____. Then, there is a **(10)** _____

celebration!

Writing

Write your own story about a special animal. Use as many words with suffixes as you can.

_____

_____

_____

_____

_____

_____

_____

Latin Roots

Many English words come from the same Latin root.
EXAMPLE: The Latin root *act* means "to do."
English words with the Latin root *act*: action, actor, react, transact, enact

Latin Root	Meaning
spec	look or see
dict	say
mot	move

Choose the word from the box that matches the meaning. Use the chart above to help you.

dictionary	motor	motion	spectator	spectacles
spectacular	remote	predict	dictator	

1. a machine that makes something move _____

2. say what will happen _____

3. movement _____

4. glasses for seeing _____

5. great to look at _____

6. one who says what to do _____

7. a book about the words we say _____

8. one who looks at something _____

9. moved far away from _____

Name _____   Date _____

Greek and Latin Roots

Many words in English come from Greek and Latin roots.
EXAMPLE: biography – a written history of a person's life
from the Greek words **bios** meaning "life" and **graphein** meaning "to write"

GREEK ROOTS	
Word	**Meaning**
metron	measure
bios	life
graphein	to write
tele	far away
hydra	water
skopein	look at
chronos	time

LATIN ROOTS	
Word	**Meaning**
vorare	to eat
omnis	all
herba	plant
centum	hundred

Choose the word from the box that matches the meaning.

omnivore	telegraph	telescope	centimeter
chronometer	hydroscope	herbivore	

1. This allows you to write to people far away. _____

2. This word means "one who eats only plants." _____

3. This word means "one who eats both plants and meat."

_____

4. This allows you to look at something under water.

_____

5. This is a unit of measurement that is $\frac{1}{100}$ of a meter.

_____

6. This allows you to measure time very accurately.

_____

7. This allows you to look at something far away. _____

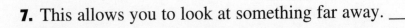

Prefixes, Suffixes, and Root Words

Many English words are made of a combination of prefixes, suffixes, and root words. Knowing the meanings of the different parts of a word can help you find the meaning of the word.

EXAMPLE:
reactor = one who does something again
prefix **re** = again
root **act** = to do
suffix **or** = one who

Prefix	Meaning
de	to remove
im	within, into
im	not
in	into
mono	one
un	not

Root	Meaning
aequalis	like
amicus	friend
imaginare	to picture in one's mind
inflatus	to blow
mergere	to dip
patiens	to endure
quietus	freedom from noise
segregare	to separate
sperare	to hope
tonus	sound

Suffix	Meaning
able	can do or can be done
er	more
er, or	one who
ion	state, quality
less	without
ly	in the manner of
tion	the state of

Use the charts to write the meanings of the words.

1. quietly _____

2. monotone _____

3. immersion _____

4. imagination _____

5. segregation _____

6. equally _____

7. despair _____

8. impatient _____

9. amiably _____

10. inflatable _____

Homophones

Homophones are words that sound the same but have different meanings and usually different spellings.
EXAMPLES: it's, its   their, there, and they're
It's means "it is." **It's** a nice day.
Its means "belonging to it." The dog hurt **its** leg.
Their means "belonging to them." That is **their** house.
There means "in or at that place." Put it **there**.
They're means "they are." **They're** going to the game.

Write *it's* or *its* to complete each sentence.

1. The team starts _____ practice at noon.

2. The coach says _____ necessary to practice.

3. I don't believe the players think _____ fun to practice.

4. Others say _____ exciting to watch the game from the sidelines.

5. The team is proud of _____ record.

6. If the team does _____ job, it will win.

7. I think _____ still a month until the championship game.

8. The team thinks _____ chance for winning the championship is good.

9. However, _____ too early to know for sure.

Circle the correct homophone in each sentence.

10. (There, Their, They're) is no reason to believe something is wrong.

11. (There, Their, They're) only a few minutes late.

12. I'm sure (there, their, they're) fine and will be here soon.

13. You know (there, their, they're) habits.

14. Wherever they go, they get (there, their, they're) late.

15. (There, Their, They're) families are like that, too.

16. I don't understand why (there, their, they're) always late.

17. Maybe (there, their, they're) clocks are wrong!

More Homophones

Remember that **homophones** are words that sound the same but have different meanings and usually different spellings.
EXAMPLES: to, two, too   write, right   hear, here
To means "toward" or "to do something." Go **to** the store.
Two means "the number 2." Buy **two** gallons of milk.
Too means "also" or "more than enough." It's **too** hot.
Write means "to put words or numbers onto paper."
Did you **write** the letter?
Right means "correct" or "the opposite of left."
Turn **right** at the corner.
Hear means "listen." Didn't you **hear** me?
Here means "in this place." Meet me **here** in one hour.

Write to, two, or too to complete each sentence.

1. It was _____ years ago that José and I went on vacation _____ the mountains.

2. We thought about going back last year, _____, but we decided not _____.

3. We both thought going _____ the beach would be more fun.

4. Since only _____ of us were going, we hoped we'd meet more people.

Write right or write to complete each sentence.

5. I'll _____ directions for finding my house.

6. You'll need a map to find the _____ roads.

7. Go ten miles, and turn _____ at the bridge.

8. You're on the _____ road if you pass the mall.

Write hear or here to complete each sentence.

9. "I can't _____ you because of the music," shouted Alana. "Why did we come _____ to talk? I can't _____ a word you're saying!" she yelled.

10. "Let's get out of _____," said Peter.

Reading and Writing Homophones

Choose the homophone that correctly completes the sentence. Write it on the line. Then, write a sentence using the other homophone.

1. (knows, nose) Fern _____ that her uncle and Lurvy take good care of Wilbur.

   _____

2. (there, their) Homer Zuckerman and Lurvy do _____ best to take care of the pig.

   _____

3. (mane, main) The animals tell Wilbur that he might be the _____ course at the Christmas dinner.

   _____

4. (some, sum) The first message Charlotte weaves is " _____ pig!"

   _____

5. (week, weak) When Lurvy first sees the web, he feels _____.

   _____

6. (here, hear) Mr. Zuckerman tells his wife that a sign has occurred right _____ on the farm.

   _____

7. (hole, whole) The _____ farm covered lots of land.

   _____

8. (rose, rows) Homer and Lurvy plowed the fields into _____.

   _____

9. (knew, new) Wilbur _____ that Charlotte was his best friend.

   _____

10. (died, dyed) Everyone was sad that Charlotte had _____.

   _____

Name _____ Date _____

Words from Spanish

Many English words come from other languages. One language is Spanish.
EXAMPLE: rodeo   The most exciting part of the **rodeo** is bullriding.

Use the clues to identify the English word that comes from Spanish. Write the English words on the lines.

 1. This word comes from the Spanish *lagarto.* _____

 2. This word comes from the Spanish *patata.* _____

 3. This word comes from the Spanish *corcho.* _____

 4. This word comes from the Spanish *mosca.* _____

 5. This word comes from the Spanish *lazo.* _____

Find other words that come from Spanish. Write them on the lines with their English words. Use the English words in a sentence.

_____

_____

_____

_____

_____

_____

_____

_____

_____

_____

Words from Native American Languages

Many English words also come from Native American languages.
EXAMPLE: skunk, from the Algonquian word *segôgw*

Use the clues to identify each English word that comes from a Native American language. Write the English words on the lines.

1. This word comes from the Algonquian *arakun*, meaning "scratcher."

_____

2. This word comes from the Algonquian word that names a soft leather slipper first worn by Native Americans. _____

3. This word, from the Sioux Indian language, names a cone-shaped tent used by Indians of the Great Plains. _____

4. This word, from the Choctaw Indian language, names the state directly north of Texas. _____

5. This word comes from the Eastern Abenaki *mos*, meaning "a large deer with huge antlers." _____

Look at a map of the United States and Canada. See how many city, state, province, and river names you can find that come from Native American languages. You may use the dictionary or encyclopedia for help. Write the names on the lines below.

_____

_____

_____

_____

_____

_____

_____

_____

_____

More Words from Other Languages

Many words we use in English come from countries and
cultures all around the world.

EXAMPLES: **pizza** and **spaghetti** come from Italian

parka comes from Russian

khaki comes from Hindi

Choose the word from the box that matches its description.

| bagel | piano | shampoo | cosmonaut |

1. This word for a special kind of soap comes from Hindi, a language spoken in

   India. _____

2. The name for this ring-shaped roll comes from a Yiddish word.

   _____

3. This word comes from the Russian word for *astronaut*. _____

4. This is a musical instrument whose name comes from an Italian word for *soft*.

   _____

**The names of many American states and cities come from languages other than
English. Write each place name beside its meaning.**

| Baton Rouge | Minnesota | Colorado | Los Angeles |

5. This state's name comes from the Sioux words for "sky-tinted waters,"

   minni sota. _____

6. This Louisiana city's name comes from the French words for "red stick."

   _____

7. This California city received its name from the Spanish words for "the angels."

   _____

Name _____ Date _____

Fun with Context Clues

Read the sentences. Use context clues to decide what the words in dark print would mean if they were real words. Then, explain why your meanings make sense.

1. Johnny goes into the **frammelhyser**. He looks at all the gifts and finally buys one for his sister.

   meaning: _____

   explanation: _____

2. While Johnny is buying the gift, he notices a colorful, eye-catching **wrythromb**. It announces a writing contest to be held soon.

   meaning: _____

   explanation: _____

3. The **plymort** for the best entry is a new bicycle.

   meaning: _____

   explanation: _____

4. "Katie needs a new bicycle," Johnny thinks. "Maybe I can **daffle** the bicycle and give it to her!"

   meaning: _____

   explanation: _____

5. "I'll write an exciting **valskur** about the time I hit a home run!" Johnny decides.

   meaning: _____

   explanation: _____

Fun with Parts of Speech

Work with a partner. Ask your partner to give you a word that is the part of speech to go in the blank. Then read the story to see if it makes sense.

Mario's Plant

I know that Mario likes unusual plants, but his newest one is downright

_____. Every ten days it drops an _____
      (adjective)   **(noun)**

of leaves onto the floor, which Mario and I have to sweep up. Then, it

_____ all its leaves back. I helped Mario search through many
      (verb)

books to find a _____ explanation for this. After searching for
                           (adjective)

three weeks, however, we are still _____.
                                           (adjective)

Julie's Costume

Julie was completely _____ about what to wear to the
                              (adjective)

costume party. Then, she _____ a bright idea! Since her
                              (verb)

favorite food was salad and her favorite animal was the rabbit, she thought that a giant

carrot would be the most _____ _____.
                            (adjective)   **(noun)**

Julie described her costume to her mother, who _____
                                          (verb)

patiently to this _____ explanation. She said that Julie should
                          (adjective)

_____ win a prize, but she wasn't sure for what.
      (adverb)

Vocabulary Skills, Grade 4, Answer Key

pages 4–5
1. A, 2. D, 3. A, 4. C,
5. D, 6. D, 7. D, 8. B,
9. A, 10. C, 11. B, 12. C,
13. B, 14. D, 15. C,
16. D, 17. B, 18. A,
19. A, 20. B

pages 6–7
1. D, 2. B, 3. B, 4. C,
5. D, 6. B, 7. D, 8. C,
9. A, 10. C, 11. A, 12. C,
13. A, 14. C, 15. A,
16. D, 17. B, 18. A,
19. A, 20. D

pages 8–9
1. D, 2. C, 3. A, 4. C,
5. B, 6. D, 7. A, 8. D,
9. B, 10. D, 11. D, 12. B,
13. C, 14. A, 15. C,
16. B, 17. D, 18. B,
19. D, 20. B

page 10
1. lumbered, 2. shriveled,
3. ransacked, 4. herbs,
5. stunned, 6. urgently

page 11
Base Words:
Sentences will vary.
1. shrivel, 2. urgent,
3. lumber, 4. ransack,
5. herb, 6. stun
Dictionary Skills:
1. herb, 2. lumber,
3. ransack, 4. shrivel,
5. stun, 6. urgent

page 12
1. lumbered, 2. shriveled,
3. stunned, 4. ransacked,
5. urgently, 6. herbs

page 13
1. translation, 2. breeds,
3. passersby, 4. rambles,
5. abandoned,
6. companion

page 14
Across: 1. passersby,
4. companion, 6. breeds
Down: 2. abandoned,
3. rambles, 5. translation

page 15
Sentences may vary.
1. The passersby had no
idea what treasures lay
inside the dusty
bookstore.
2. The house had been
abandoned for many
years.
3. Many breeds of dogs
were at the dog show.
4. The morning glory vine
rambles across the porch.
5. His companion
remained by his side
throughout all his
troubles.
6. What translation will I
need to be able to
understand this foreign
language?

page 16
1. sentinel, 2. rodents,
3. era, 4. sculpted,
5. mantle, 6. reside

page 17
Synonyms:
1. B, 2. F, 3. A, 4. E,
5. C, 6. D
Dictionary Skills:
1. A, 2. B, 3. D

page 18
1. rodents, 2. reside,
3. sculpted, 4. sentinel,
5. mantle, 6. era

page 19
1. exhaustion, 2. volcano,
3. lava, 4. stampede,
5. interrupted, 6. erupts

page 20
Word Groups:
1. volcano, 2. exhaustion,
3. interrupted,
4. stampede, 5. erupts
Dictionary Skills:
Answers may vary
depending on the
dictionary used.
1. la-va, 2. stam-pede,
3. e-rupts, 4. vol-ca-no,
5. ex-haus-tion,
6. in-ter-rupt-ed

page 21
1. stampede, 2. lava,
3. exhaustion, 4. erupts,
5. interrupted, 6. volcano

page 22
1. brand, 2. gauchos,
3. manes, 4. siesta,
5. lasso, 6. hooves

page 23
1. hooves, 2. lasso,
3. siesta, 4. brand,
5. gaucho, 6. mane

page 24
Dictionary Skills:
1. brand, 2. gaucho,
3. hoof, 4. lasso, 5. mane,
6. siesta
Word Wise:
1. lasso, 2. brand,
3. gauchos, 4. hooves,
5. siesta, 6. manes
Answer: Argentina

pages 25–26
1. A, 2. B, 3. C, 4. A,
5. D, 6. B, 7. D, 8. B,
9. A, 10. D, 11. C, 12. D,
13. B, 14. D, 15. D,
16. A, 17. D, 18. C,
19. B, 20. B

page 27
1. opportunities,
2. cautiously, 3. settlers,
4. determination,
5. frontier, 6. succeed,
7. supply

page 28
1. B, 2. A, 3. A, 4. B,
5. A, 6. B

page 29
Sentences may vary.
1. We drove cautiously to
the top of the mountain.
2. We felt as if we were
at the edge of the frontier.
3. We felt lucky because
few people have the
opportunities to see such
great views.
4. We had to bring plenty
of water and food because
we knew this area might
not supply us with enough.
5. We were the first
settlers to this area.
6. She showed such
determination that we
knew she could succeed.

page 30
1. emigrants,
2. occupations,
3. convinced,
4. prospecting,
5. citizenship,
6. foreigners,
7. hardships

page 31
Antonyms:
1. emigrants,
2. hardships,
3. convinced,
4. foreigners,
5. occupations
Dictionary Skills:
Answers may vary
depending on the
dictionary used.
1. con-vinced,
2. pros-pect-ing,
3. cit-i-zen-ship,
4. oc-cu-pa-tions,
5. for-eign-ers,
6. hard-ships,
7. em-i-grants

page 32
1. convinced,
2. citizenship,
3. prospecting,
4. occupations,
5. hardships,
6. Emigrants,
7. foreigners

page 33
1. indifferent,
2. miniature,
3. dreaded, 4. expression,
5. assured, 6. appeal,
7. custom

page 34
Synonyms:
1. custom, 2. appeal,
3. dreaded, 4. assured,
5. miniature, 6. indifferent,
7. expression
Dictionary Skills:
1. appeal, 2. assured,
3. custom, 4. dreaded,
5. expression,
6. indifferent, 7. miniature

page 35
1. miniature,
2. indifferent,
3. expression, 4. assured,
5. custom, 6. appeal,
7. dreaded

page 36
1. lantern, 2. deed,
3. acres, 4. loophole,
5. foreclose, 6. mischief,
7. startling

page 37
Compound Words:
1–6. Order of answers
may vary.
loophole, everything,
headline, newspaper,
foreclose, hardship
Dictionary Skills:
1. D, 2. C, 3. B, 4. B,
5. A

page 38
1. lantern, 2. foreclose,
3. acres, 4. deed,
5. startling, 6. loophole,
7. mischief

page 39
1. avoided, 2. cowering,
3. endurance, 4. fury,
5. intensity, 6. probing,
7. suspicious

page 40
1. intensity, 2. probing,
3. endurance, 4. avoided,
5. suspicious, 6. fury,
7. cowering

page 41
Dictionary Skills:
1. suspicious,
2. endurance, 3. fury,
4. avoided, 5. intensity
Word Wise:
1. cowering, 2. avoided,
3. endurance, 4. probing,
5. suspicious

pages 42–43
1. A, 2. D, 3. B, 4. C,
5. D, 6. A, 7. D, 8. B,
9. A, 10. C, 11. C, 12. A,
13. C, 14. B, 15. D,
16. B, 17. C, 18. A,
19. A, 20. C

page 44
1. adapt, 2. mesquite,
3. stalks, 4. habitat,
5. scrubland, 6. content,
7. wandering

page 45
Classifying:
1. mesquite, 2. adapt,
wandering, stalks,
3. scrubland, habitat,
4. content
Dictionary Skills:
Answers may vary
depending on the
dictionary used.
1. mes-quite, 2. hab-i-tat,
3. stalks, 4. con-tent,
5. a-dapt, 6. scrub-land,
7. wan-der-ing

page 46
1. mesquite, 2. stalks,
3. adapt, 4. habitat,
5. scrubland, 6. content,
7. wandering
Answer: nature walk

page 47
1. environment, 2. exotic,
3. immediately, 4. nectar,
5. preserve, 6. rare,
7. substance

page 48
1. synonyms,
2. antonyms,
3. synonyms,
4. antonyms,
5. antonyms,
6. synonyms,
7. antonyms

page 49
Dictionary Skills:
1. substance; 2,
2. nectar; 2, 3. preserve;
2, 4. exotic; 3, 5. rare; 1,
6. environment; 4,
7. immediately; 5
Word Wise:
1. substance, 2. preserve,
3. rare, 4. nectar,
5. exotic, 6. immediately,
7. environment

page 50
1. remarkable,
2. species, 3. coral reefs,
4. submerged, 5. obvious,
6. skeletons, 7. organisms

page 51
Word Groups:
1. skeletons,
2. submerged,
3. remarkable, 4. species,
5. coral reefs,
6. organisms
Dictionary Skills:
1. B, 2. B, 3. D

page 52
Sentences will vary.

page 53
1. gills, 2. cast, 3. weight,
4. hovering, 5. trout,
6. reel, 7. exclaimed

page 54
1. B, 2. A, 3. B, 4. A,
5. B, 6. A

page 55
1. trout, 2. cast, 3. reel,
4. hovering, 5. exclaimed,
6. weight, 7. gills

page 56
1. mimics, 2. techniques,
3. enables,
4. surroundings,
5. noticeable, 6. survival,
7. resemble

page 57
Base Words:
Sentences will vary.
1. survive, 2. notice,
3. mimic, 4. surround,
5. enable
Dictionary Skills:
1. enable, 2. mimic,
3. notice, 4. surround,
5. survive

page 58
Sentences may vary.
1. The powerful flashlight enables Marcus to see into the dark cave.
2. Without a steady source of food, the pioneers had much less chance of survival on the frontier.
3. The chameleon mimics colors found in nature.
4. Each animal has its own special techniques for training its young.
5. Melinda was completely lost. She didn't recognize her surroundings.
6. Even though Joe had spilled his drink on his jeans, the spot wasn't noticeable.
7. The daughters resemble their mother so much that sometimes it's hard to tell them apart!

pages 59–60
1. B, 2. A, 3. D, 4. A,
5. A, 6. C, 7. A, 8. C,
9. C, 10. A, 11. D, 12. D,
13. C, 14. B, 15. A,
16. A, 17. A, 18. A,
19. D, 20. B

page 61
1. effects, 2. inspiration,
3. prodigies, 4. omit,
5. impressions,
6. stimulates,
7. exhibition

page 62
Base Words:
Sentences will vary.
1. effect, 2. inspire,
3. exhibit, 4. stimulate,
5. prodigy, 6. impress
Dictionary Skills:
1. effect, 2. exhibit,
3. impress, 4. inspire,
5. prodigy, 6. stimulate

page 63
1. prodigies,
2. exhibition,
3. stimulates, 4. omit,
5. inspiration, 6. effects,
7. impressions

page 64
1. rhythm, 2. tempo,
3. choreography,
4. jubilation, 5. heritage,
6. debut, 7. dignity

page 65
Answers may vary.
Possible answers:
What dance shows about a culture: dignity, heritage
How and when dance is performed: choreography, debut
Elements of dance: tempo, rhythm
What dance makes dancers and the audience feel: jubilation

page 66
Sentences may vary.
1. The audience felt jubilation watching the dancers perform.
2. The tempo of the music made us want to get up and dance.
3. Dance helps us celebrate our heritage.
4. It was hard to resist the rhythm of the music.
5. Tanika was very nervous about her debut.
6. She wanted the dance to show the dignity of her people.
7. We thought she had created wonderful choreography for the music.

page 67
1. constantly,
2. delicate, 3. artificial,
4. distinguished,
5. monotony, 6. splendid,
7. composed

page 68
Antonyms:
1. splendid or distinguished,
2. distinguished or splendid, 3. composed,
4. delicate, 5. artificial,
6. monotony,
7. constantly
Dictionary Skills:
Answers may vary depending on the dictionary used.
1. splen-did,
2. dis-tin-guished,
3. con-stant-ly,
4. del-i-cate,
5. mo-not-o-ny,
6. com-posed,
7. ar-ti-fi-cial

page 69
1. constantly,
2. composed,
3. distinguished,
4. splendid, 5. artificial,
6. delicate, 7. monotony

page 70
1. acknowledges,
2. temper, 3. considerate,
4. praise, 5. advise,
6. bountiful,
7. silhouetted

page 71
1. B, 2. A, 3. A, 4. B,
5. B, 6. A

page 72
1. temper, 2. considerate,
3. bountiful,
4. silhouetted,
5. praise, 6. advise,
7. acknowledges

page 73
1. sheepishly, 2. ad-lib,
3. triumphantly, 4. UFO,
5. monotones,
6. immersion, 7. device

page 74
Pictures will vary.

page 75
Answers may vary.
1. Ben Stein has become famous for speaking in monotones.
2. She soaked her tired feet in an immersion bath.
3. The young man sheepishly accepted the prize for the best apple pie.
4. She knew how to ad-lib about many different topics.
5. When I saw something streaking across the night sky, I thought it might be a UFO.
6. The team returned triumphantly after winning the game.
7. That new device will help people travel more safely.

pages 76–77
1. C, 2. D, 3. C, 4. D,
5. C, 6. D, 7. A, 8. C,
9. B, 10. A, 11. C, 12. D,
13. B, 14. D, 15. D, 16. D

page 78
1. disappear,
2. unconcerned,
3. unaware, 4. discover,
5. unharmed, 6. dislike,
7. disagree,
8. misunderstood,
9. misuse, 10. recreate,
11. relive, 12. misjudged,
13. react

page 79
1. unfair, 2. returned,
3. unable,
4. misunderstood,
5. preplanned,
6. impatiently, 7. repay,
8. unhappy,
9. displeased,
10. returned

page 80
1. disregarded,
2. unknown or unfamiliar,
3. unfamiliar,
4. disappearing, 5. return,
6. unwisely, 7. impossible

page 81
1. successful, 2. tireless,
3. effortless, 4. careless,
5. meaningful, 6. endless,
7. worthless, 8. joyless,
9. without color,
10. without bottom,
11. full of sorrow,
12. full of beauty,
13. without flavor

page 82
1. stormy, 2. visitor,
3. politely, 4. musical,
5. wonderful, 6. magical,
7. remarkable,
8. unbelievable,
9. actually, 10. friendship

page 83
1. helpful or successful,
2. handler, 3. lovable,
4. partnership,
5. willingly,
6. confidently, 7. tireless,
8. carefully, 9. successful,
10. joyful

page 84
1. motor, 2. predict,
3. motion, 4. spectacles,
5. spectacular, 6. dictator,
7. dictionary, 8. spectator,
9. remote

page 85
1. telegraph,
2. herbivore,
3. omnivore,
4. hydroscope,
5. centimeter,
6. chronometer,
7. telescope

page 86
Meanings may vary.
1. in the manner of being free from noise, 2. one sound, 3. the state or quality of being dipped into, 4. the state or quality or picturing in one's mind, 5. the state or quality of being separate, 6. in the manner of being alike, 7. to remove hope, 8. not able to endure, 9. in the manner of being a friend, 10. can be blown up

page 87
1. its, 2. it's, 3. it's,
4. it's, 5. its, 6. its, 7. it's,
8. its, 9. it's, 10. There,
11. They're, 12. they're,
13. their, 14. there,
15. Their, 16. they're,
17. their

page 88
1. two; to, 2. too; to,
3. to, 4. two, 5. write,
6. right, 7. right, 8. right,
9. hear; here; hear,
10. here

page 89
Sentences will vary.
1. knows, 2. their,
3. main, 4. Some,
5. weak, 6. here,
7. whole, 8. rows,
9. knew, 10. died

page 90
1. alligator, 2. potato,
3. cork, 4. mosquito,
5. lasso

page 91
1. raccoon, 2. moccasin,
3. tepee, 4. Oklahoma,
5. moose

page 92
1. shampoo, 2. bagel,
3. cosmonaut, 4. piano,
5. Minnesota,
6. Baton Rouge,
7. Los Angeles

page 93
Answers will vary.

page 94
Answers will vary.